THE TORCH AND THE SWORD

RICK JOYNER

THE TORCH AND THE SWORD

RICK JOYNER

MorningStar Publications

A DIVISION OF MORNINGSTAR FELLOWSHIP CHURCH

P.O. Box 440

Wilkesboro, NC 28697

The Torch and the Sword
Copyright © 2003 by Rick Joyner
Third Printing, 2004

Distributed by MorningStar Publications, Inc., a division of MorningStar Fellowship Church
P.O. Box 440, Wilkesboro, NC 28697

International Standard Book Number: 1-929371-36-5

MorningStar's website: www.morningstarministries.org
For information call 1-800-542-0278.

Cover Design by Tim Dahn
Book Layout by Sharon Whitby

Unless otherwise indicated, all Scripture quotations are taken from the New American Standard Bible, copyright © 1960, 1962, 1963, 1968, 1971, 1973, 1974, 1977 by The Lockman Foundation. Italics in Scripture are for emphasis only.

CONTENTS

INTRODUCTION

THIS BOOK IS A COMPILATION of fourteen years of prophetic visions, dreams, and experiences that began in 1988 and continued through 2002. It was not until 2002 that I saw how these fit together, forming an important part of the message that was first published in *The Final Quest* and continued in *The Call*. This book includes experiences that came both before and after those written in the previous two volumes.

You may wonder why the Lord would give prophetic revelation in such a jumbled timeline. I often wonder the same thing. However, a message in these visions helped me to understand the reason. Also, if you become a student of biblical prophecy, you will quickly learn that the events foretold in a single chapter of Scripture can jump back and forth thousands of years. It is my opinion that the Lord does this kind of thing to keep us dependent on His Holy Spirit, not only for the revelation, but for the interpretation and application as well.

Understanding prophecy has obviously been placed intentionally beyond the realm of human science or wisdom. This can often be disconcerting and discouraging to those who are inclined to depend on their own abilities in their search for understanding. To the true God seeker, the mysteries are a part of the glorious, ultimate quest— the great adventure that seeking God is supposed to be.

The quest to know God and His ways is full of mystery. There are keys to unlocking these mysteries such as faith, devotion to truth, integrity, and sanctification. However, these are not to earn gifts and revelation from Him, but to separate those who are true worshipers of a holy God from those who are just seeking knowledge.

Even so, we are completely dependent on the Lord's willingness to show us something before we can understand it the way that is intended. Fortunately, one of the greatest of His promises is that if we will seek Him, we will find Him. It is my hope as you read this compilation of experiences that you will gain the understanding of His ways. Even more, I hope you are drawn to experience Him for yourself with the end result being that you love Him more and are closer to Him.

THE PROPHETIC PACKAGE

It has always been interesting to me that more people ask how I receive the things I write about than ask me about the issues which they address. This is not wrong. In fact, there is merit to under-standing the package in which revelation comes. This is because often the package is a part of the message. For this reason, I included in this introduction and occasionally in the text of the book, the way in which they came to me.

Very often I am also asked for more personal information about myself. This too is a fair request, as we are exhorted **"to know them which labor among you"** (I Thessalonians 5:12 KJV). I think there are some issues and events in my personal life that can help give more understanding to the prophetic experiences, so I have also included those in this introduction. However, if you are not interested in this kind of information, I encourage you to go straight to Chapter One where the vision begins.

A PERSONAL JOURNEY

Most of the dreams, visions, and prophetic experiences included in this volume were personal messages to me, so I have written them in first person just the way they came. Therefore, understanding some of the parts of my personal journey at the time they came may be helpful to understanding the message.

Even so, I have not included anything that I believe was intended to be just a personal message for me. As I was repeatedly told in these experiences, I am but one of many who are called to the things addressed in them. It is in this same way that the events throughout Scripture, which happened to individuals and were personal messages for them or personal letters to specific groups, also speak to all Christians. If these apply to you or your situation, you should freely take them personally.

To lay a brief foundation for the messages contained in this book, in 1980 I left full-time ministry because I felt my personal relationship to the Lord had become shallow. I felt too superficial in my faith and experience to be leading others. I was deeply convicted by Galatians 1:15-16:

> **"But when He who had set me apart, even from my mother's womb, and called me through His grace, was pleased**
>
> **to reveal His Son in me, that I might preach Him..."**

I was beginning to understand that even though God had called me to the ministry I was attempting, I had confused His calling with His commissioning. Because of this, I started in the ministry prematurely. The Lord had been revealed *"to me,"* but not **"in me"** which Paul explained had to happen before he went forth to preach.

Paul was also preaching **"Him,"** Jesus. My ministry had been mostly devoted to principles and formulas for success—spiritual and Christian success, but still my message was more about us than Him. I felt like the men of Athens, worshiping an **"unknown God" (Acts 17:25)**. Most of my knowledge of God had come from other people rather than having been revealed to me by the Spirit, which Paul acknowledged as being crucial for his own ministry.

All of this combined to make me a very shallow and ineffective minister of the gospel, and compelled me to resign from the ministry and seek secular employment until I felt the Lord had truly been revealed **"in me."**

As a licensed Airline Transport Pilot, I took a flying job. This usually required me to fly a couple of hours a day and then spend many hours sitting in airports and hotel rooms. This gave me plenty of time for studying and seeking the Lord. I was often able to spend as much as forty hours a week in study and prayer.

Then the corporation I was working for moved its plane, and suddenly my job ended. As I began to search for another job, I was surprised to receive a word from the Lord that I needed to return to the ministry full-time. In fact, I was shown that even though I was as superficial and inadequate as I had seen myself, I had overreacted and the Lord did not intend for me to leave the ministry. This word came in 1982.

Still, by no means did I feel ready to go back into "ministry," but rather felt that it would probably take me many more years to be adequate. When I shared the word with my wife and best friend, they too felt this was not the course I should take at that time. I was easily persuaded to reject the call because of my feelings of inadequacy, so when an opportunity came for me to start an air charter business, I took it.

I consider starting that business to have been the biggest mistake of my life, but I did learn a lot through it that has helped me greatly since. The Lord is in the redemption business and He will use even our mistakes for our good. However, it is always better not to make the mistakes and I am in no way implying that we should make mistakes so that good can come. As the apostle Paul said—that kind of thinking is a foolishness which brings judgment. Even so, we can be thankful that He will use even our mistakes for our good if we really love Him and are called according to His purpose. So good came of it, but it would have been even better had I obeyed His call instead of taking a seven-year diversion.

FLYING HIGH, THEN CRASHING

The air charter business became successful very quickly. Soon the business included a flight school, aircraft sales, maintenance, insurance, and the oversight of the busiest airport in the state I was living in at the time. This all left me with little time for study and seeking the Lord. Though I learned a great deal about business and management, these were mostly wasted years spiritually.

The more successful I became, the emptier I felt inside. Even so, I was very close to having a net worth which would enable me to retire completely and devote myself to the ministry again without needing any outside support. This is how I justified being so driven to keep building the business and making more money.

While on a hunting trip in 1986, I was sitting in a field alone. Suddenly, I felt the presence of the Lord and He began to speak to me, asking me to lay my business "on the altar." I noted that He said this was *my* business instead of His, as I had always claimed.

To my surprise the Lord had also been offended by my vision of being able to make enough money to support myself in ministry so that I would never have to take up an offering. He was offended because this implied He was not capable of taking care of those who were in His service. He showed me that this was rooted more in my pride than in a noble devotion. I "gave" the Lord my business and asked Him to do with it whatever pleased Him.

Immediately the business that I had worked so hard to build began to collapse. Soon I was in bankruptcy court, having lost a small fortune. I was able to sell our assets, including our dream home and property to pay our debts. When it was all over, I owned a car and had a couple of thousand dollars. I felt I had been a failure in ministry, and now a failure in business.

Some who were the closest to me were faithful in reminding me that I was a failure, but I hardly needed reminders. It was the low point of my life.

I knew I was called to a ministry and did want to one day be devoted to it full-time, but I did not want to enter the ministry as a failure but rather as a success. I was ashamed that I felt I had nothing to offer the Lord, but this too was pride. I had proven in all ways to be both weak and foolish. I know the Scripture that says this is usually the kind of person He calls, but there is a big difference in being a failure in business (financially) and being a failure spiritually where people could be hurt. I was still reticent to return to the ministry where others could be hurt by a failure.

Then one week in early 1987, two people from different parts of the country, who I knew did not know each other, came to me and gave me the same word from the Lord—if I did not return to the ministry immediately, He would give my commission to someone else. I did not know what my commission was, but it shook me enough to enable me to lay everything aside and return to the ministry. My apparent weakness and foolishness would just make me have to trust the Lord more, which is of course exactly what He wanted.

I had self-published my first book, *There Were Two Trees in the Garden,* in 1985 while still in business. The only advertising for this book had been by word of mouth, but by 1987, distribution was growing rapidly. This was bringing in quite a few invitations to speak in churches and at conferences. After the word to return to ministry came, I decided to take some of these offers. I especially wanted to get a sense for what was happening in the body of Christ at that time, as I had been out of circulation for seven years.

After just a couple of trips, I came home quite discouraged by the seemingly overwhelming lack of purpose and direction in the church. This lack of direction in the church did not help me to understand my own purpose and direction for ministry either. As I was praying about this situation, I had a two and a half-day prophetic experience in which I was shown a panorama of coming events (which I published in my book entitled *The Harvest*). That vision imparted to me a great hope for the future, and the church, which has given considerable purpose and direction to my ministry since.

A New Level of Prophetic Encounters

During the two and a half days in which I was given this extensive vision of the coming harvest, I felt I had received more prophetic revelation than I had in any other seven-year period of my life. In those two and a half days, I felt the time I had missed in the seven years that I had been distracted from my ministry was made up. In a very real way, the Lord made up for me **"the years the locust have eaten" (Joel 2:25 NIV)**. It also made me appreciate the value of prophetic experiences like I never had before.

Within months of having this vision, I started meeting other people who had some of the most remarkable prophetic gifts of which I had ever seen or heard, except in Scripture. Many of these people would become my lifelong friends. One of these was Bob Jones.

When I met Bob, he shared a couple of dreams that he had about me which described my plight. He gave me some answers to where I was headed, all with amazing clarity. There were even details in these dreams about my family of which I was not aware, but later were confirmed to be true.

In the coming months, Bob called and gave me words or shared dreams which were incredibly specific and detailed, and then they would come to pass in the most amazing ways. This was more wonderful than can be described, imparting to me a sense of being in the will of the Lord like I never felt before in my life. Every day became an amazing and wonderful adventure. I was convinced this was the way the Christian life was supposed to be!

Then Bob gave me a word that I was to have a visitation from the Lord in October of 1988. He said that in this visitation I would receive a commission which would establish me on my course. I naturally waited with great anticipation, but October passed with no visitation. I assumed that Bob had missed something and just continued my increasingly busy schedule.

THE GREAT REBUKE

In March, I was scheduled to meet Bob in Louisiana to visit a few churches there. Before leaving I received a word from the Lord that I had become too busy and I was already five months behind in what He had given me to do that year. I determined that after this next trip I would slow down.

Before meeting Bob, I went to Texas to do some television programs with James Robison. After taping the programs, James and I were sitting in his office talking. Suddenly he started chastising me for being too busy. Having just heard the same rebuke myself, I took his counsel even more seriously.

After leaving James' office, I asked for the Lord's forgiveness. He spoke, reminding me that I was five months behind in finishing a project that He had given me to do. He also reminded me that it was five months since the promised visitation and this was the reason I had not received the commission yet. He said if I would repent and go home, He would visit me.

I called and left a message for Bob that I was not going to meet him in Louisiana. I called my wife and told her the same thing, as she was visiting her parents in Slidell, Louisiana, and was planning to come over with the kids for the meetings. I then left for my home in Charlotte, North Carolina.

A VISITATION

When I arrived at our empty house, I began praying and seeking the Lord. I wanted more clarity about how I had come so far off track in such a short period of time. All He said was for me to go to bed because He was going to visit me that night. I assumed He meant in a dream, but I was so excited that I did not think sleep would be possible. Even so, I turned off all of the lights in the house and went to bed.

The Lord must have put me to sleep because I do not even remember lying down. In the middle of the night, I suddenly awoke feeling a presence in the house. I was surprised since it seemed like all of the lights were on, and yet I remembered turning them all off. I wondered if one of my neighbors had come in, not knowing I was home. Suddenly the Lord walked into my room. There were no lights on in the house. The light was coming from Him.

I was terrified. I was grasping my pillow and wanted to get up, but was not able to. He walked over to me and placed His hands on my shoulders. I felt power building up within me like electricity. It was not painful as much as uncomfortable because a great pressure was building up inside. Soon the pressure became so great that I was afraid I was going to explode. When I did not think I could take it any longer, He took His hands off and the power receded. He did this over and over, each time taking His hands off right when I thought I was about to die.

Then He stood up and started to walk out of the room. I was concerned that He had not said anything to me and I did not know what this experience had meant. He turned just before going through the door and said, "Bob Jones will explain this to you." I could not help but wonder why He did not just explain it to me, Himself. The next thing I remember was waking up in the morning.

I lay in bed for a while remembering everything that had happened. I started to wonder if He had really come, or if it had been just a dream. When I sat up and reached for my clothes, I felt a surge of power go through me just like when He had laid His hands on my shoulders. Electricity arced from my hands to the post of the metal bed. I knew then that it had been real and not just a dream.

For a few minutes I was afraid to touch anything for fear that I might electrocute myself! I felt so much power inside that it was scary. When the power finally receded, I got up and dressed.

During the morning, the surges of power would go through me every hour or so. I did not know if I wanted them to stop or continue because I did not really understand what it was. I could hardly do anything but sit in awe. Finally, I went next door to visit my neighbors, Harry and Louise Bizzell. As soon as I walked through the door, Harry looked at me and said, "You had a visitation!"

I do not know if I just looked that scary or if Harry discerned it, but he knew. This made me feel free enough to tell him about it. I told him the one thing that bothered me was that I could not remember how many times the Lord had laid hands on me and I knew this was important. Harry suggested that I call Bob Jones since the Lord had said he would explain it to me.

I had been hesitant to call Bob because I wanted him to hear from the Lord and call me. However, at Harry's suggestion I decided to call him just to ask how things were going in Louisiana, but was determined not to even give him a hint about the visitation. I wanted to be sure that anything he received was from the Lord.

When I talked to Bob on the phone he said that everything was going fine. However, when he had tried to pray that morning he was amazed by "how the heavenlies were stirred up." He said the only time he had ever seen them that stirred up "was when Jesus passed through to visit someone."

I still did not tell Bob anything, but was encouraged greatly by the way the heavens were stirred up. It was just another confirmation to me that the visit was real and not just a dream. It should not have mattered because a visit from the Lord in a dream is real, but for some reason it was important to me then.

The next day Bob called me. He had received a visit from an angel who had told him about my visitation from the Lord and my commission. He told me why the Lord had laid hands on me *five times*, and other details, giving me Scriptures which further explained it, as well as some things about my future.

I acknowledged everything and thanked him. I was surprised when he rebuked me for having such a lack of faith, which required him to have to confirm things like this. I did not know if Bob was joking or not, but when I laughed at his rebuke, I noticed he did not.

THE MESSAGE

What the Lord had imparted to me was a commission to help release the five equipping ministries listed in Ephesians Four to the church, which are essential for her to fulfill her last day ministry. This is central to my purpose and is therefore a part of every message I give, every book I write, and nearly every thought I think. There are few things more fulfilling to me than seeing someone begin walking in one of these ministries, and truly becoming one who "equips the saints to do the work of the ministry."

Another part of the message had to do with walking in His power and calling and commissioning those who are called "the messengers of power." These are also the ones which Enoch prophesied about, and they are soon going to be released upon the earth. When this happens, the works of the Lord will be seen throughout the earth in a way in which they never have been before.

I have seen some extraordinary works of power from time to time, but I am just now starting to move toward walking in this commission. Also, the Lord never showed me that I would be one of these messengers of power. I would surely like to be, but I was simply given the commission to awaken and help prepare those who would walk in this. I was also told that I am only one of many who are called to do this.

What the Lord had given me to do, which was already five months behind in completing, was to finish the book **The Harvest.** This was the message He had given to me the year before in the two and a half-day experience, which I described previously. I resolved to finish it as quickly as possible.

This book went on to surpass **There Were Two Trees in the Garden** in distribution, but over the next couple of years the Lord showed me how it would have reached far more people had it been released on time. Being on time with messages was a basic mandate the Lord gave me for starting MorningStar Publications and Ministries, which came in Matthew 24:45-47:

Who then is the faithful and sensible slave whom his master put in charge of his household to give them their food at the proper time?

Blessed is that slave whom his master finds so doing when he comes.

Truly I say to you, that he will put him in charge of all his possessions.

The Lord wants His household to get their food **"at the proper time"** and already timing was one of my great weaknesses—I think it still is. I tend to get so busy, mostly in ministry, that I miss important directives, messages, meetings, and getting the food out on time, which He has given to us for His household.

I should have returned to the ministry when He first called me rather than starting the air charter service. I had almost lost my commission to someone else because of my reticence and feelings of inadequacy. Then I had overreacted and became so busy that I almost missed my commission because I was doing too much. There is a ditch on either side of the path of life and I had fallen into it on each side!

The reason I am sharing some of these personal things is because they are common mistakes for Christians, especially those in positions of leadership in the church. It is also something that must be corrected or the consequences will be more costly as we approach the end of this age. These are primary reasons most Christians are not walking in their calling and not fulfilling their destiny and purpose. They are missing in both of the same ways that I almost did.

Many miss because they are too hesitant to start. Others get into ministry and quickly become so busy doing things for the Lord that they fail to draw close to Him. A successful Christian life will not be based so much on how much work we have done, but rather on how close to the Lord we have become, and how obedient we have been.

It is not possible to walk as we are called without a personal encounter with the Lord every day. We need a holy addiction to His presence so that He becomes more important to us than oxygen. I do not consider to have attained this yet myself, but it is my greatest pursuit.

THE COMMISSION

When I told Jack Deere about the visitation I had in early 1989, he remarked that he could not wait to see me praying for the sick. He felt that the power imparted to me from this visit was going to release many miracles. I too could not wait. However, the results were not very impressive. In fact, I felt so un-anointed praying for the sick that I was afraid if I prayed for someone who was crippled that they might leave both crippled and blind!

I then rationalized that the prophetic gifts in me would go to another level. They did not. In fact, I could not tell that I had any more anointing to do anything. Even so, it was during this same year that revelations did come which would lead our ministry toward some of its ultimate purposes. Without realizing it until recently, it was during that year I was given the foundational understanding of my life's message.

Not long after this, Bob Jones told me that I was going to receive another visitation from the Lord and another commission. It would come to me on the first of spring when I was in London. Much of what you are going to read about in this book came during that experience.

A CALLING TO PREPARE THE WAY

In late 1989, we were able to lease an estate in Charlotte, North Carolina as a base for MorningStar Publications and Ministries.

We moved there in early 1990. Roger Hedgspeth and Steve and Angie Thompson became our first staff members. Shortly after them, Leonard Jones joined us as a worship leader, even though we did not have any meetings yet that required one, and did not have any planned.

As typical of where the ministry was at the time, we found a little shack in the woods, fixed it up for Leonard, and just told him to do what he does before the Lord. Leonard was a faithful, hard worker, showing up every day and staying long hours. What he did was worship. As he worshiped, he also did some composing. When he first played what he was writing, I was stunned. I had never heard music like it before (we are yet to record this music, but hopefully it will be done soon). I was also impressed that Leonard was finding others who needed such an opportunity. I knew if we could find them, greater things than we ever expected would be released from them.

I determined to continue reducing my travel schedule to devote myself to establishing the ministry in North Carolina. Steve Thompson, Robin McMillan, Leonard Jones, and I started what we called School of the Spirit (which was quickly dubbed "SOS" meetings). Amazing things started happening from the first meeting.

These meetings were stirring up gifts in a lot of people, so Steve Thompson asked if he could hold some training meetings for people who felt called to the prophetic ministry. I agreed and was amazed at how quickly extraordinary gifts were being released in numerous people, many of whom had never been used in that way previously. Soon, all of the believers around us began to be confident that they could personally know the voice of the Lord and be used by Him to do exploits. It started to feel like New Testament church life.

THE VISION

When the Lord called me to return to the ministry in 1982, He had shown me a teaching center and prophetic community. He said that when the prophets and teachers learned to worship Him together as they had at Antioch, we would again be able to release apostolic authority on the earth.

For the succeeding years, I was shown many things about the coming last day ministry and the last day church, that it would truly be an apostolic church. I was shown how the Lord would be revealed through His people before He returned to rule the earth. I saw a church on earth which really was without spot—pure, holy, and full of such grace and power that the nations would all be in awe of her. Her message of the coming Kingdom would shake every kingdom on the earth.

My ultimate part in helping to prepare the church for her calling revolved around the teaching center and prophetic community. It would be a place from which prophetic words and teachings would be distributed around the world. To see this come to pass soon became a primary devotion. Even so, I knew the timing for this had to be right and that the most important things usually take the longest time to unfold. I knew I would have to stay focused as well as patient.

As of this writing, this community is still in the formative stages. I expect it to take a few more years before even the foundation is completed. In fact, I think my primary job is to lay a foundation for some things that others are called to build upon. This is important to understand if you are to grasp the message of this book.

It is my calling to summon those who will live to do the will of God. They will live in a way which will forever be a testimony that truth is greater than any lie and that love is stronger than death. At the same time, mankind is learning for sure that anything done without the Lord will ultimately lead to the most terrible disaster. They will also see the most wonderful consequences from things that are done in obedience to Him.

I have been promised that I will see at least the beginning of the most extraordinary move of God since God Himself walked the earth. And this move will prepare for Him to walk the earth once again. If you are a Christian, it is your calling and destiny to be a part of this.

A SECOND VISITATION

The second visitation was in 1995 after Bob Jones visited our base in Charlotte. After we had finished one of our SOS meetings and we were sitting in our kitchen the first night, Bob was looking around as if there was something specific he wanted to find. He then asked me where the building was with the loading docks and the sign that said, "No empty boxes." I told him our warehouse had a loading dock and I would show it to him the next day. He said he had seen it in a vision and that it was important.

Later, Bob asked me if I had planned my trip to London yet. I had in fact just accepted an invitation to go to London to speak at a conference. I was surprised that Bob knew about this. He then said that I needed to be there on the first day of spring. I thought about my schedule and realized that I was in fact going to be in London on the first day of spring. I asked Bob why I needed to be there at that time and he reminded me of the word he had given me years before, which I had forgotten. A little perturbed at my forgetfulness, he started asking me a series of questions.

First, he asked me how long we had lived on that property. I answered that it had been five years. Then he asked me how long it had been since he had given me the word about London. It turned out to have been five years. He asked me how long we had been publishing *The Morning Star Journal*. It had been five years. He asked me how many children I had. Our fifth child had just been born.

He then asked me Amber's age. (She was our third child and Bob had prophesied her birth two years before she was born, having given us the date on which she would be born, August 8, 1990, and her weight, which was exactly 8 pounds). Amber was five years old. All of these dates related to her birth because she was to be a sign of a new beginning coming to the church.

He then asked how long we had been holding the School of the Spirit meetings. It had been five years. Finally he said that I was going to London to receive a commission from the Lord in which I would receive five things.

"NO EMPTY BOXES"

The next day I took Bob to our warehouse, loading dock, and offices. He said he had seen our place in a vision, but this was not it. He kept looking for a sign that said, "No empty boxes," but we had no such sign.

We had been looking for a larger building for our meetings, so we decided to take Bob by one which we were close to leasing. As soon as we were near, Bob perked up. When we walked inside, he was sure it was the building he had seen in his vision. He wanted to see the loading dock. As we were looking around, we went through a door which on the other side had a sign that read "No empty boxes." Not far away was the loading dock just as Bob had seen it in the vision. We signed the lease right away and this became the home of MorningStar Fellowship Church in Charlotte.

Remembering the time the Lord had laid hands on me five times, I left on this trip to London with great anticipation. As I sat in my hotel room in London on the first of spring, it was a dreary, rainy day.

I was a bit depressed because of some things I had seen in a ministry that had hosted our meetings. Then suddenly I was caught up into another realm.

It was in this experience that the Lord gave me the five things, which are written about in this book. Over the next eight years, He added to my understanding of each one. Recently, in a series of prophetic experiences I was taken back to revisit the same places. The second visit was in some ways even more powerful than the first. When the Lord speaks two times like this, it often speaks of the level of importance in them. That is when I also determined that these experiences needed to be written. This message was not just for me, but is for many who are about to be awakened to an awesome destiny. These things will soon begin to unfold.

SUMMARY

Again, I have written these visions in first person because that is the way they came. I was in these experiences. I have been told by some that the message would be more palatable if I had written them in third person or as an allegory. This may be true, but I did not feel this would be honest or accurate. I tried to write them just as I experienced them.

I have also seen many change their minds who had a hard time believing that the Lord still speaks to people in this way, mostly because they started having the same kind of experiences. We can expect much more of this as we proceed toward the end of this age, which is clearly stated in Acts 2:17-18:

"In the last days," God says, "I will pour out my Spirit on all people. Your sons and daughters will prophesy, your young men will see visions, your old men will dream dreams.

Even on my servants, both men and women, I will pour out my Spirit in those days, and they will prophesy" (NIV).

You simply cannot believe we are coming to the last days without understanding that there will be a dramatic increase of prophetic revelations and experiences. In fact, every time the Holy Spirit is poured out there are accompanying dreams, visions, and prophecy.

The text in Acts 2, which is taken from Joel 2, emphasizes this because in the last days the release of prophetic revelation obviously happens on a much more expansive scale. I have watched with great interest and sometimes amusement, as many who do not believe that these experiences are for today start having them! Like it or not they are coming. As this Scripture states, it is one of the signs that we are truly coming to the last days.

Even so, one of the reasons these experiences will become so common as we proceed toward the end of this age is because we are going to need them. They are not for our entertainment or just to make our services better. They are crucial for our guidance and we are going to need more specific guidance in the times ahead. It is this conviction which has compelled me to be far more open in writing about the nature of the experiences that have come to me.

I have two personal goals which compel me in almost all I do. One is to become so obedient to Christ that literally all of my thoughts are obedient to Him. The second is that I want to be more at home in the heavenly realm than the earthly, just as the apostle Paul said about himself.

I live for the day when Christians can sit on the side of a mountain with an entire army seeking them and have perfect peace because they can see that those who are with us are more than those who are with our enemies. I want to see prophetic ministry restored to the body of Christ so that even our enemies will say what they did about Israel, "There are prophets there who know what the kings of this world say in our innermost chambers!" I believe this is the heritage of the body of Christ. This is supposed to be normal Christianity.

Paul wrote in II Corinthians 3:7-8, **"But if the ministry of death, in letters engraved on stones, came with glory, so that the sons of Israel could not look intently at the face of Moses because of the glory of his face, fading as it was, how shall the ministry of the Spirit fail to be even more with glory?"**

This states that the glory we are supposed to be experiencing in the New Covenant is greater than what Moses experienced! Moses met with the Lord face to face, and even had to put a veil over his own face because of the glory that reflected from him. We are supposed to be experiencing something greater than that!

One of the ultimate questions of our time should be: "Where is the glory?" One thing we can count on before the end of this age is that the glory of the Lord will be manifested in His people, just as we are promised in Isaiah 60:1-3:

"Arise, shine; for your light has come, and the glory of the Lord has risen upon you.

"For behold, darkness will cover the earth, and deep darkness the peoples; but the Lord will rise upon you, and His glory will appear upon you.

"Nations will come to your light, and kings to the brightness of your rising."

At the very time darkness is covering the earth and deep darkness the peoples, the glory of the Lord is rising on His people and appearing on them. These are the times to which we are coming. This is what I have seen in almost every vision, dream, or prophetic experience that I have written about—darkness and conflict, glory and magnificence. I would prefer to see only the glory, but the two are coming together and we must see and understand them both.

Accordingly, the body of Christ is about to go through a metamorphosis. It has been like a caterpillar crawling along the ground, but it is about to emerge into a glorious butterfly which soars above the earth. The church that is about to arise will be more at home in the heavenly realm than the earthly.

The kinds of experiences I am writing about will not seem strange to that church, and those who are going to be a part of it will soon hear a clear trumpet call, which is revealed in Revelation 4:1-2:

After these things I looked, and behold, a door standing open in heaven, and the first voice which I had heard, like the sound of a trumpet speaking with me, said, "Come up here, and I will show you what must take place after these things."

Immediately I was in the Spirit; and behold, a throne was standing in heaven, and One sitting on the throne.

There is a door standing open in heaven with an invitation for us to go through it. Those who answer this call will be caught up into the Spirit, with the result that they will always be seeing the One who sits on the throne. This is the ultimate purpose of all true, prophetic revelation—seeing the glorious, risen Christ and the authority that He now has over all.

There is a difference between believing in our minds and believing in our hearts. We may well know and believe the doctrine that Jesus is now above all rule and authority and dominion, but if we really believed this in our hearts, our lives would be radically different.

As Romans 10:10 states, **"for with the heart man believes, resulting in righteousness..."**

One of the primary results of any experience is to change concepts into heart beliefs. This is going to be the result of the prophetic revelation which will be poured out **"in the last days."** This will bring about a transformation of the church that is as radical as the worm becoming a butterfly. For this reason I pray that you are not satisfied with just reading about my dreams and visions, but that you will have your own.

This vision is not complete and is still unfolding. I ended this book at a place that seems like the middle of the story because it is. There is much more to come. However, the rest is so extensive that it will require another book. Even so, the message contained in this book is enough for us to deal with for some time to come.

This is not a fantasy. True Christianity is the greatest adventure that anyone can ever have on this earth. True church life, the way it was intended to be, is a supernatural experience. It is life from another realm beyond this earth that brings true life to the earth. My prayer is that the message of this book will open those who read it to have life in a greater reality—a life which testifies that heaven is real and that our King is seated on a throne that is above all others.

Rick Joyner

1

THE TORCH

I SAT IN MY HOTEL ROOM IN LONDON. I felt restless and thought about walking to Buckingham Palace which was just a few blocks away. Even though I knew I was in the right place at the right time, it had been one of my most difficult ministry trips ever.

I began thinking about the prophecy that had foretold this trip. I lay my head back in the chair to rest for a moment. Suddenly, I was in another world.

I was standing on a beach. Water was gently lapping at my feet. I thought I must be dreaming, but I knew I was not asleep. I looked at the sky which was brilliant with color. It was like no sunset or sunrise that I had ever seen. I then pondered why I could not tell if it was a sunrise or a sunset.

Then I noticed the air. It was more than just clear and fresh. With each breath I felt I was being rejuvenated, my mind was being quickened, and my thoughts were becoming increasingly sharp and clear.

I looked at the mountains in the distance and began to study them. They seemed to be at least fifty miles away, but maybe much farther. The air was so clear that it was hard to tell. I love mountains and have seen some of the world's most majestic, but these were more wonderful than any I had ever seen. They were like great fortress walls which exuded strength and purpose, yet they were also hospitable and inviting.

I then looked down at the water between the mountains and me and wondered if there was a way around it so that I could go to the mountains. As far away as they were, I was drawn to them like a magnet and wanted to go to them immediately.

I felt compelled to look more closely at the water. It too was crystal clear with just a hint of blue and a stunning contrast to the sky. I wondered if there could possibly be a more perfect place. In a strange way it seemed like home, like the place I belonged. I was coming alive in a way that was more than wonderful. It was like waking up from a dream into reality, but a much more wonderful one.

Then I noticed a figure walking toward me on the beach. I could see from the distance that He was carrying a torch. It gave off light which was the same color as the sky. I knew immediately that it was the Lord. I could tell by the way He walked, with purpose but not in a hurry. He is never in a hurry because time submits to Him. As He got closer, I could see that He wore a white robe with a golden sash that was tied in the front. The hem at the base of His garment had a pattern of gold, as did the end of His sleeves.

"It is sunset and sunrise," He said. "A sunrise in one place is a sunset in another. You live in the sunset of one age and the dawning of another. That is why you are here, to learn about the end of the age in which you are now and the beginning of the one which is dawning."

As He drew close, He extended the torch to me indicating that I should take it.

"This is yours," He said. "I started this fire, but you must keep it going."

As I took the torch I was surprised that it was so light, which made me think it must also be fragile.

"It is neither light nor fragile," the Lord said, answering my thoughts. "It has more substance and weight than the earth itself. This is the light of My presence. If I was not close to you, you could not hold it. If you drift from My presence, it will become heavy. If you drift very far from Me, you will have to lay it down. Then someone else will pick it up and carry it. It is yours to carry for as long as you stay close to Me."

As I continued to study the torch the Lord continued, "This torch breathes the air of heaven, not earth. No power on earth can put it out if the torchbearer walks with Me in this realm. Its brightness and power depend on the life of the torchbearer, and on how close he stays to Me.

I was still looking at the torch when the Lord began to walk down the beach. He had only taken a couple of steps when I noticed the torch was getting heavy. I quickly caught up to Him. Then another voice behind us started speaking.

"Even the torch itself can distract you from following Him."

I turned to see a middle-aged man dressed in simple monk's garb. He had a serious but cheerful face. He continued talking as we all walked.

"In your times there will be as many who carry this torch as in all of the times before you. You will know the torchbearers when you meet them. You must encourage and help one another. Because none of you can stand alone, you must join with other torchbearers. When you do, you will be able to overcome the power of the evil that will confront you. You can set people, cities, and even nations free with the light of this torch."

I then noticed that the torch was breathing—it was alive! I grabbed it with both hands and a surge of power flowed through me as if I had completed some kind of circuit. My vision increased, my mind became even sharper, and I felt my strength growing. I could not comprehend how anyone could lay aside such a treasure.

"You have not yet felt the pain of it," the Lord interjected. "I uphold the universe with My Word. It is My Word that enables you to hold this torch. This torch is the light of My presence and it is also what you call 'a movement.' I Am the Living Truth, and truth which is living is always moving. In the beginning the Holy Spirit moved and He has not stopped moving. Life moves."

The monk who was walking with us added, "In Him we live and *move*. The Holy Spirit is always moving. When He moved upon the formless void, the chaos, He brought forth life. That is His purpose—to turn the chaos that evil has made in the world into the life of a new creation. When you move with the Spirit life, creativity will be the air your spirit breathes."

"Who are you?" I asked.

"I am the one you call 'Thomas à Kempis.'"

"I am honored," I said. "I know your writings well. They sustained me through some dark times. In fact, overall I think they are some of the most powerful I have ever found written outside of Scripture."

Thomas continued as if he had not even heard my remarks. "The times of great darkness will soon come upon the earth. There was darkness on the earth in my time, but not such as you are about to see. Remember, you will never be in the dark if you stay close to the Lord. The torch that you carry has been the source of every true movement of the Spirit. The leaders of these movements were all torchbearers. The movements that stopped moving and therefore stopped living, did so because the torch was laid aside.

If you are going to endure to the end, you must stay close to the Source of this light and fire. He is moving and you must not stop moving."

The Lord motioned for Thomas to come beside Him. As He put His hand on Thomas' shoulder, His affection for him was obvious.

"Men thought of Thomas as a humble laborer, one to cook, wash dishes, and weed the gardens, but he too carried this torch. From his post of washing dishes, he became more powerful than kings or emperors. He prophesied to millions over generations. Even today My message goes forth from his writings to help prepare the coming ones. You can be more powerful washing dishes and staying close to Me than you would be leading armies or nations but drifting from Me."

As we continued to walk, Thomas began to speak again.

"This torch is offered to all of His messengers. Only a few have carried it and fewer still have carried it for very long. Not many have learned to abide in His presence. If you will stay close to Him, you will take what you see and feel here with you and impart it to many others. Many will be drawn to Him by this. If you take this torch, and then lay it down, you can also be used to do much evil."

"How would anyone who has seen the Lord and carried this torch of His presence be used to do evil?" I protested.

"This torch will give its bearer great influence. Those who have carried it and then laid it down, often did so because they began to esteem the influence of the torch more than His presence. As they drifted from Him, the torch became too heavy for them and they laid it aside, substituting their own words for His Words. This is how the doctrines and traditions of men began to eclipse the influence of His Spirit over men. This has happened to every movement until now. Do you think you can do better than all of the other torchbearers?"

I felt the seriousness of this warning. I knew very well my tendencies to drift from seeking the Lord and staying close to Him. I also knew my pride and presumption at times to think that my thoughts were His thoughts and my words were His Words.

Even in the glory of His presence, as we walked a chill came over me. Once I was given this torch my failures would be compounded, with many more people affected. I thought about my previous failures in ministry, and then my failure in business. Each one had been a little more devastating. Now my ministry was growing again. Could I carry the weight of this responsibility? In almost every way that counted, everything which I had started in the past had ended as a failure. "Would it be any different this time?" I thought.

The Lord looked at me in a way that conveyed both kindness and forgiveness, but at the same time I felt the severity of the warning I was there to receive.

"My Spirit will go with you and convict you of your tendency to drift from Me. Even so, you must follow My Spirit. Even the torchbearers will not be forced to follow Me. All will fall who do not love Me more than sin and wickedness. All will fall who do not love the truth more than they love the praises of men. If you love Me and My truth more than the idols that the world now worships, you will not fall. This will be your daily choice—to follow Me or serve idols that can easily eclipse your affection for Me."

I gripped the torch much tighter. As I did I felt so much energy flowing through me that it was as if every cell in my body was awakened and ready to spring forward. I thought of Romans 8:11, **"But if the Spirit of Him who raised Jesus from the dead dwells in you, He who raised Christ Jesus from the dead will also give life to your mortal bodies through His Spirit who indwells you."** Being close to Him was causing my mortal body to come alive like I had never felt it before.

As I was awakened in this way, I began to realize *everything* in that place was alive—the trees and grass, but also in a strange way it seemed that the mountains themselves were alive. Even the clouds were somehow trying to speak. In a profound way it felt natural. It was right. I began to have a kind of fellowship with everything that I could see. As I drank this all in the Lord continued.

"It is now time to show the earth that heaven exists. Lower the torch to the sea."

I lowered it to the water until it touched. Then I lowered it further until it was completely submerged. The fire of the torch continued to burn brightly and even more beautifully under the water. Then the water caught on fire. Flames spread out from the torch and began to sweep toward the horizon. It did this slowly and steadily, which reminded me of the way the Lord walked. I wondered if the sea was actually composed of some kind of fuel. As I looked at it more closely, I could tell that it too was alive!

I watched as the fire burned. There was no smoke, no fumes. There was some heat but it was gentle, a kind of penetrating warmth that seemed to release even greater energy inside of me. As I stood by, it continued to increase. Soon I felt that I could leap over a house or maybe even lift one. It was an extraordinary, wonderful feeling. As I became alive I was joining a life force that gave me the strength of the whole. It was like experiencing a spiritual critical mass.

Thomas was watching me closely and soberly. He then added:

"As you abide in Him and do His will, you begin to flow with His life force which is in all of the living. In this way, as we help others to come alive, the life grows in us too. Do not fall to worshiping this life force; you will only stay on the path of life if you seek the Source of life."

I knew this was another important warning, This was the trap that many cults and new age movements had fallen into. Even so, I wanted to remember the feeling. I knew that everyone who ever tasted of this life force would be forever addicted to it, perpetually seeking it like a junky seeks his next fix. Thomas, also obviously reading my thoughts, continued:

"There is no intoxication like life itself, but remember that it is still intoxicating. Many fall under even the slightest touch of His Spirit and can become drunk in the Spirit by just a taste of this. However, the priests had to learn to stand and minister even in the presence of His glory. If you yield your body to this life, you will be drunken. If you yield your spirit, you will be quickened, strengthened, and see even more clearly. You must train the coming ones not to seek to feel good and not to become intoxicated by this power, but rather sobered, able to see clearly and function in their duty. You will have forever to feel good after you have accomplished your purpose."

The Lord turned and looked directly at me.

"You can set nations on fire with this torch. This is the same fire that Moses saw in the bush. This is the fire I sent with him to set My people free. It is what I am about to send with My messengers to again set My people free."

I looked at the fire on the water and I saw that the water was composed of multitudes of beings—people! They were on fire but they were not being consumed. They were coming alive. This was a fire that would one day cover the earth. It would consume the wood, hay, and stubble, but it would purify the gold, silver, and precious stones in every life. I thought about what the Lord said in Luke 12:49:

"I have come to cast fire upon the earth; and how I wish it were already kindled!"

I looked over at Thomas. He knew what I was thinking.

"Yes, the time has come. The fire is now kindled!"

2

THE MESSENGER

WE REMAINED BY THE BURNING SEA FOR A LONG TIME. The life, energy, and peace that I felt continued to grow. It was like a rush of joy that did not pass away, but rather increased toward a certain fullness of joy. I knew there was nothing on earth that could compare to this, yet it seemed vaguely familiar.

"You are experiencing the joy and strength that man knew before the fall," the Lord explained. "You are only beginning to experience what is actually a normal life for man, the way I created him to live."

As the flames of the sea swept over me gently, I began to recognize the feeling. It was what I had started to call "the Emmaus Road burning heart." It is the way in which our heart burns when we walk close to the Lord and He personally teaches us. I began to think of Adam, who had walked with God in the Garden, and Enoch, who had walked with God so closely that he was translated straight into heaven.

The Lord again answered my thoughts. "When I walked with Adam, I taught him about the creation and his purpose for cultivating and maintaining it. I also gave him the freedom to be creative as he cultivated it. He was created to bear My image. To bear the image of the Creator, one has to be creative. In this we had great fellowship.

"True creativity can only be found by those who walk closely to Me. It is a relationship to Me that few have experienced, but that I cherish very much. Some do this, and walk very close to Me, even though they do not know My name. They do not know that I was made flesh and walked on the earth. The time has come for all who seek Me and My ways to know My name, and to know My ways which were revealed when I walked the earth.

"When Adam walked with Me, he was in harmony with the creation and felt the energy and strength you now feel. He was so full of life that he lived almost a thousand years after sin entered him, and the discord of sin entered his soul. There is great power in life, but all life will lose its power if it does not stay close to Me.

"Enoch yearned for what Adam had lost. He walked with Me and I began to teach him like I did Adam. He discovered the source of life, walking with Me. The life became so great in him that he would have still remained on the earth if I had not brought him up to dwell with Me here. He was too full of life to die so I had to take him up.

"I am still learning about life," another voice behind me said.

I turned and there was a man standing far away in a beautiful green meadow. His voice had seemed to be much closer than he actually was. He began to walk toward us in a way similar to the Lord's walk—resolute, but unhurried. As he approached I noticed that his face was the same color as the sky, the torch, and the Lord's face. He also wore a garment similar to the Lord's. He walked up and took the torch out of my hand.

"I must bless you before you go—I must bless the torch-bearers. The purpose of every movement on the earth is to compel men to do what I did—to walk with God until they are more at home in the heavenly realm than on earth. Man was created to dwell on the earth with his body while his spirit soared into the heavens."

"Are you Enoch?" I asked.

"I am," he said as he reached over and touched my heart.

"The fire burns but what you lack is discipline and endurance. You walk adequately for short periods. Now you must learn to walk with endurance. You must resolve to walk each day in the domain over which the Lord has given you to rule. He has given you authority, but you must walk with Him in your domain. Only then will you be fruitful and multiply as you are called to do. Your domain is your garden. The path of life always leads to unity and harmony—with God first and then with all that is His. This takes strength and endurance because the whole creation is now in discord, and it opposes unity."

Enoch then took the torch and touched it to my heart. It caused a great rush of energy and power and then a joy that almost could not be contained. When he pulled it away, the fire continued to burn inside of me and the energy continued to surge in waves throughout my body. I knew I had felt this before.

"The Lord makes His messengers flames of fire. You cannot walk with God or fulfill His purpose for you on the earth unless you keep this fire burning in your heart. Lukewarmness is your deadly enemy. You must not let the fire wane by drifting from His presence. This fire that now burns in your heart must be given fuel each day. Its fuel is the atmosphere of heaven, which is the breath of God. What He breathes upon lives and what He does not breathe upon dies. Seek this life and pursue it. If you do, you will leave a trail of life where the River of Life will break out and flow. If you walk as you are called, you will help restore true life to the earth."

Enoch then took my face in his hands and just looked into my eyes. He was the very definition of graciousness. He seemed to be so saturated with joy and love that I felt he was the most like the Lord of anyone I had ever met. I felt that anyone who saw him would spend their life trying to be like him. I then realized the main reason he was looking into me was so I would look into him. I did. Then he released me and walked back in the direction from which he had come.

"Enoch has a special investment in you," the Lord said as we both watched him go. "He prophesied the coming of the mighty ones who are soon to be released on the earth. From the time he was allowed to see them he has waited for this time. You are called to help awaken these mighty ones to their destiny. When they are awakened, they will have the heart of Enoch. Their might and strength comes from this torch which Enoch first picked up and other faithful ones have kept alive on the earth.

"From among those coming, there will arise many like Abraham, Moses, Elijah, John the Baptist, Peter, Paul, and John. There will be as many as a thousand like each of the great messengers of the age that is now ending.

"After each of the torchbearers departed the earth, they left their mantles of authority to be picked up by the others. These have been divided just as Mine was at the cross. When one has a part of a mantle which comes together with one who has another part, their authority will be magnified. Many of these mantles were hidden and kept for this time. These have been reserved for those who will be My messengers in the last days.

"It is true that spiritual authority multiplies with unity. One can put a thousand to flight, but two can chase ten thousand. The unity that these last day messengers of power walk in will multiply the authority of the mantles they carry. The earth has never seen anything like what I am about to release through these messengers. They will walk in the fire of all who went before them. So now you must help them find their way and their mantles."

"Lord, here I feel I can do anything. Will I still feel this way when I return to the realm of earth?" I asked.

"No. When you return, this will all seem like a dream to you. The earth is under a shroud of fear and doubt which is growing thicker and darker. Even so, this realm is more real than the earth. Those in your time who break through the fear and doubt to walk in the power of life here will have the greatest faith, and they will be trusted with the greatest authority.

"You may only vaguely remember what you see and feel here. Even so, the yearning for what you are now experiencing has been imparted to you and this yearning will not go away. It is real and will lead you to reality.

"You can have all that you experience here again, but you too must grow up into it as you walk with Me on the earth. Only by this will you be wise and humble enough to be trusted on earth with the authority and power that you feel here. The wisdom and humility are more important than the power. Without them the power will corrupt you and you will be used for evil. It is by your wisdom and humility that you will be able to help My messengers along their way."

I turned to see Enoch again and was surprised that he had gone only a few paces back. He was watching me with a very keen interest. He had a look of resolution that bordered on ruthlessness, but was also combined with affection. Together this made him seem to be the very definition of rock solid stability. I thought of how wonderful it would be to have had a mentor like him on the earth. The Lord once again answered my thoughts:

"You are called to be like him, as are all those I am sending to prepare My messengers of power. As you see My glory in Enoch, you will be changed by it. This is what you are called to be for other torchbearers and they will be to you. You are not alone as there are many others who are called to this just as you are. However, you cannot be like him until you have walked with Me as he has. That is your whole purpose now—to walk closer to Me each day. "

I then looked up at the clouds. They were as regal as the mountains. Each one seemed precisely in its place like those an artist would use to perfectly grace a painting. In no way did they hinder or block the light or the sky, but framed it in a way which accentuated it. There was one directly above us that formed a perfect canopy. The clouds were so alive that personality exuded from them. They had purpose. I knew they were devoted to accenting as perfectly as they could the glory of everything that was around them and they were doing this for us. The clouds were so wonderfully loveable that I wished there were some way to show them to every child on the earth.

The Lord let me drink this in and then continued. "I created man to be the torchbearer for all of creation. All men have this calling and were created to walk with Me and carry the light of life. Many are called, but few are chosen. You must now go and find those who have persevered to become My chosen ones. They will keep the fire and ignite in all men the fire that man was created to have.

"You will know these chosen ones by the fire that already burns in them. They will never be content with religious practices, for they yearn for Me and the reality of this realm. Because they seek Me, I will be found by them. I will give them their heart's desire—My fellowship. I will be their inheritance.

"I will also give them greater authority than I have yet entrusted to men on the earth. They will receive this because they will have the wisdom and humility to use it. When the Day of Judgment comes, their testimony will be that they walked with Me and their fire did not dim. These are My messengers for which the whole creation has been waiting and travailing. It is time for them to awaken."

The Lord then stepped out on the water into the midst of the flames. I watched as He began walking toward the mountains. I knew I had to follow. As He walked out onto the burning sea, the torch became heavier. If I was going to continue holding the torch I would have to follow Him, but I was hesitant about trying to walk on the water. Finally I determined to step out without thinking anymore about it. When I did I was able to walk on the sea as if it were a paved road.

The fire on the sea was hot, but it did not burn me. Instead, like the torch, it seemed to be imparting energy to me. As we walked He turned and said:

"You are here because you have learned to see. To see is to evaluate and to seek understanding. This is the eye of the child. As long as you keep it I can teach and lead you.

"Those who walk with Me grow in the strength that is in Me. I gave all men the capacity for this, to grow in both natural and supernatural strength. Those who do not walk with Me have a void in their soul for this supernatural strength. Those who do not walk with Me turn to the evil one for power to fill the void in their heart.

"I give My power to those who are wise and mature enough to use it. The evil one gives his power to those who are foolish and immature enough to be used by it. The time is coming upon the earth when all must choose to walk with Me or be taken over by the power of a greater evil which has yet to be known on the earth."

As we walked waves of fire spread out from us on the sea as if we were a wind blowing. When the Lord pointed in a direction, the flames intensified in the direction that He was pointing. I tried pointing and it did the same. Then the Lord stopped and turned to look at me.

"I have a fire to cast upon the earth that has now been kindled. Pray for My fire to come. It will purify the earth. Pray for it to consume the chaff and to purify My chosen ones. I gave authority over the earth to man and therefore I must be asked before I will move on the earth. This is the great purpose of those who walk on the earth, to know Me and My will. Then they can ask for My will to be done on earth just as it is done here in heaven, and it will be done. What you will now see here is so you will know My will on the earth for your time."

Suddenly I was standing in a valley.

3

THE HORSE AND THE GIRL

AS I SURVEYED THE VALLEY, THE FIRST THING that caught my attention was a beautiful stream flowing through the middle. It was a natural setting yet in some way it seemed wonderfully manicured. It was so seemingly perfect that I could not tell if I was still in the realm of heaven or back on the earth.

Then I heard noise above me and on both sides. It sounded like many thousands of stomping feet. It was an alarming sound, especially in such a peaceful setting. I knew right away that something was not right. A great multitude appeared at the top of the mountains all around. It was an army of some type. As I watched they began to descend from the top moving slowly, even tentatively, but relentlessly.

I began to feel very strongly that this was an evil army with evil intent. Then thousands of vultures appeared as a cloud above them, circling as if waiting for the slaughter. I was appalled by what they would do to this beautiful place, not to mention afraid for myself as I was obviously hemmed in by this evil horde.

"What are you going to do about it?" a voice behind me asked.

I turned to see who was speaking and saw a large, white stallion. It was beautiful, with muscles rippling even as it stood still. It had intelligence in its eyes that I had never seen in an animal before, so I wondered if it had spoken.

"What *can* I do about it?" I asked.

"I see you are a torchbearer. This horse is for you," the voice continued. "You must learn to ride it if you are going to help stop the evil horde that is coming."

"Is there time to learn to ride a horse?" I asked looking around for the owner of the voice, since it was now clear that the horse was not speaking.

"There is still time."

Then a young girl who seemed to be ten to twelve years old stepped from behind the horse. She was dressed in what appeared to be a school uniform, but it was covered with silver and gold armor that was worn and battered. A sword was strapped to her belt. She was thin with a beautiful face and brilliant blue eyes which were set with a fierce, penetrating focus. She exuded a boldness and confidence with a childlike purity that was stunning in its nobility.

"I am here to teach you how to ride," the girl said. "We have time," she repeated as if trying to calm me.

I was captivated by this little girl, but still agitated by the huge dark force that was descending on us. I marveled at how calm she was. I wondered if she was just too young to understand what such a horde from hell would do to her and this place. However, as I looked at her it was obvious that she had both experience and intelligence beyond her years.

"I understand much more than you think," she replied as if my thoughts had been spoken out loud. "I am here to fight with you, but first you must learn to ride this horse. We do have time, but not time to waste. We must get started."

"Let's get started then," I said, not wanting to waste a second. "I know how to ride a horse. Is there anything special I need to know to ride this one?" I asked.

"I don't know," she answered. "I have never ridden a horse."

"But I thought you just said you were here to teach me how to ride. How are you going to teach me if you have never ridden a horse yourself?"

"You will learn by teaching me. You will not be fully trusted with this horse until I have my own and can ride it as well as you do. You also must understand that this is not like any horse you have ridden before."

"Tell me all that you know," I replied. "Can we drink from this stream?" I asked, feeling thirsty and weak.

"Of course. That is why it is here."

I reached up and touched the reins on the horse. I then gently pulled and it started to follow me without a hint of resistance. When we reached the bank of the stream, I reached down and brought a sip of water to my lips. Immediately my eyes brightened and my mind became clear.

As I continued to drink, I felt stronger. I gently nudged the horse forward and it knelt down on its knees and drank. I had never seen a horse do that. The little girl did the same getting down on her knees to drink. I decided to do the same and drank my fill.

"Fear makes you weak," the girl said when she had finished.

"You're a very wise little girl," I responded thinking how truly extraordinary this child was. "How do you know so much and how do you know about this torch?"

Before she could answer, the increased noise from above caused us both to look up. There was obvious confusion in the ranks of the evil host. My eyes were so sharp now from the water that I could make out some of the banners over the different divisions.

The banners that I could see were named after different philosophies, religions, and strange mystical teachings, which I had heard about but I was not very familiar with. There were other banners but they were too small or far off for me to read.

As we continued to watch, the confusion increased until some of the divisions started fighting with each other. A huge cloud of dust was rising and battles were breaking out in all directions. Soon the entire horde was disappearing back over the tops of the mountains. However, they did not go far because I could still hear them and see the dust rising from a great commotion which was obviously going on among them. Even so, it seemed we were safe for a while.

"That is why we still have time," the little girl explained. "Demons hate each other as much as they hate us. They can't march together for very long before they start fighting each other. The only thing that can keep them unified is a battle with us. Their fear of us is stronger than their jealousy of each other. That is why we must be ready to defeat them when we fight. When we fight we must destroy them completely."

"You talk as if you are a seasoned warrior," I said, examining her armor. "Please tell me more."

"I have already watched well meaning but foolish people try to fight the evil ones before they were strong enough to defeat them. This only made the enemy stronger, and more unified. Battles that are not fought until there is a complete victory always result in our losing more ground to the enemy.

"Even though it was before my time, I was told that we once had control over much of this country. Now we are surrounded in this little valley. The next time we fight we must win or all will be lost."

Then she looked at me with her penetrating blue eyes. They were like the blue of the hottest part of a fire. "Retreat is not an option! We have nowhere left to go!" she declared with more seriousness than I had ever seen in such a young child.

This startled me as I had been looking around to see if there was any way of escape.

"How old are you?" I inquired. "How do you know so much?"

"I am twelve but I have been fighting since I was five. I have learned much in the battles, but my wisdom comes from this river. This is the River of Life. It gives the life which transforms experience into wisdom, the vision that is true."

"This is a beautiful stream, but hardly a river! This can't be the River of Life!" I protested.

"It is. It is small here because it is always as large or small as its demand. Not many will come here to drink anymore because they have to get past the evil ones who have seized the high places. Most would rather drink from the polluted streams which are not under attack than the true living waters that are now always under attack. Few are thirsty enough to fight for this, but there is nothing worth fighting for more that I know of."

"Did you have to fight your way here?" I asked.

"I did. I came right down that path," she said pointing to a place at the far end of the valley behind me.

"How did you get past the evil army?" I inquired. "Are there still gaps that you can get through?"

"No. They have us completely surrounded now. But anyone with the courage to keep moving even when they are attacked can make it through their ranks. I chose the weakest part of their army and walked right through the middle of it."

"What was the weakest part? And how did you know it was weak?"

"There was a large division called 'Ridicule.' I chose to walk through it because I knew they could not really hurt me. I was told when they saw my resolve that they would give way before me, and they did. They raved and screamed insults and obscenities, but they parted and let me pass. I blocked all of their shots with my shield and was not even wounded."

"Who told you that you could do that?"

"My mother."

"Is she here, too?" I asked.

"No."

"Where is she?"

"She didn't make it through. When we were passing through the ridicule, she stopped and said she was going back to get more people and lead them through. She said she would join me later. I don't think she will though."

"Why not?"

"She taught me very well, but she could not do what she taught me to do. I saw her waver from the insults and ridicule. She went back to get more people because she needs the approval of people.

No one can make it through who cares too much about what others think of them."

"Can she make it in some other way?"

"It is possible, but going through the ridicule is by far the easiest way. In fact, when she hesitated and started to retreat she was quickly overcome. She then began ridiculing me with the rest of them. Once you begin to retreat before the evil ones, you are easy prey for them. She is now one of their prisoners."

"I'm sorry. I know you must miss her. She was at least a great teacher. She did a great job teaching you."

"Thank you. I do miss her. It has been very lonely here, but it is still better than being out there under the influence of that evil horde."

I watched the little girl drift far off in her thoughts. Then quickly she snapped back to the conversation.

"I knew when we started it would be hard for her and that she probably could not make it. I also knew I could not let that stop me. The only hope for her to ever get free and be able to drink from this stream is by me not stopping until I have fulfilled my destiny."

After a pause, she continued, "I have not given up on her, but myself and others like me are the only hope for people like her. We are here to defeat that evil horde and set its prisoners free. I do believe the time will come when she will drink with me at this stream—she and many others until this is a great river again. It will then flow to the sea and bring life to all."

If there are many others like you, then I have no trouble believing that you will win the victory. Have you met others like yourself who have this vision and resolve to do this?" I asked.

"I think I have met some, but we keep getting separated. I know from my dreams that there are many more and I will meet them soon. That's why you are here. I have seen you in my dreams too."

"Tell me, what did you see about me?"

"Well, I did not see you specifically, but I saw the coming of the torchbearers. At first there were just a few, and then more and more kept coming. I too will one day be given a torch to carry. In fact, many of the torchbearers are quite young."

As she was speaking a large division of the evil army crested the top of the mountain and started down much more rapidly and in relatively good order. We watched transfixed as it advanced almost a third of the way down the mountain. Then it was attacked from the rear by another one of the evil divisions. Soon it sounded like several more joined in the assault on it.

The advance was stopped at that point while most of the column turned around to fight. However, a large part of this group remained at the point of its greatest advance and started setting up defenses, which quickly started to appear like a fortress.

As I looked at the little girl I saw her nervous for the first time. I then noticed that the horse was also agitated.

"What do we do now?" I asked, surprised that I was asking a little girl for instructions.

Without answering the girl knelt down at the stream again and drank with purpose. Soon she regained her composure, but her attention was still fixed on the fortress that was quickly being built. The horse had become so agitated that I was afraid it was going to run.

I walked over to take its reins and was surprised by how it looked me straight in the eyes. I tried to stay as calm as I could because I felt if he sensed fear in me, he would certainly bolt. He let me take the reins and lead him back to the stream. It was not as easy to get him to drink, but he did. Then he calmed down. I drank and the peace and joy again filled my being, while my vision grew stronger.

"What do we do now?" I asked again. "Have you seen anything in your dreams about this?"

"I did not see this in a dream, but I have seen this happen before. If we do not act soon, we will lose this valley."

Then she looked straight at me to be sure I would hear what she was about to say.

"Whenever I am asked what to do I always turn to the river first and drink. Then I pray, as we must do now. I have been in two other places where this river ran and both were taken over by the enemy. We must not let this happen here. We must fight this time," she said looking at me kind of skeptically. "I will fight even if I have to do it alone. I don't think there is anywhere else left to go where this river flows."

"It is very noble to want to fight and to even be willing to fight alone" I replied, "but how can just the two of us stand against so many?"

She did not answer me, but started praying. I listened for just a few minutes. Her requests were concise and to the point. She did not try to explain anything to God. She mostly asked for the Holy Spirit, courage, wisdom, and power to defeat the enemy.

She then prayed for her mother and other loved ones who were captives of the evil horde. She asked for specific places to be retaken from the enemy. It was the prayer of a seasoned warrior who had seen many battles and did not want to waste time or words. It was also like a conversation with her friend. It was so moving that I did not believe the Lord could possibly reject her requests. When she ended, she looked up at me. All I could say was "Amen."

"You asked how we could defeat such a huge army. Why couldn't we? We have the Lord on our side."

"I understand, but how were the others lost that you fought for? What can we do this time differently? And are you sure there are no other streams like this one?"

"The way that they have all been lost is by retreating. I will not retreat again. I will not listen to those who speak of 'strategic retreats' or any other kind. I am going to stand even if I have to do it alone. I also think that we lost them because there were too many of us."

"How could there have been too many when you are fighting against so many?" I asked, not doubting her as much as feeling that the answer to this was important.

"It is better to have a few who are in unity than many who are divided and who do not have a single, focused vision. Many of those who were with us before seldom drank from the stream and I hardly ever heard them pray. I felt they would not last long and I was right. Such people are more of a detriment when the battle begins. Our leaders had to spend more time trying to encourage them than fighting.

"Many of the weak ones even turned on us. I determined before the next battle that I would not encourage anyone too much, trying to get them to stay and fight. If they want to leave, then they should because we would be better off. There is also something else very important that we have never had before that we must have to win."

"What is that?"

"The torch. This water is the truth and we must have and love it enough to be willing to die for it. But the torch is like the presence of the Lord here with us. When I am close to you and the torch, I feel Him!

"There is no greater encouragement than feeling His presence with us. If we had carried the torch before, I don't think our leaders would have had to spend so much time encouraging the people, nor do I think they would have been so weak.

"And yes, there are other streams like this one, but there is only one river. It rises out of the earth in different places like this. I have been told that they used to be very common. Now there are not many streams because so few have been willing to fight for them. I am not even sure there are any more like this one.

"Right now we need more true warriors, not more streams. I have heard that every time new streams break out, they are quickly lost because so few are willing to fight for them. This is why we need torchbearers."

"I know what you are saying is true, but I still don't know why more people won't fight to defend them. Are they always as hopelessly outnumbered as we are at this time?"

"I do not believe in the word 'hopeless,' but I think those who seek this river are always outnumbered. Like I said, I don't think the numbers are that important. We need more warriors, but we need more who are true warriors.

"I've heard some say that digging hidden wells is better than seeking the river because they are not as big a target for the enemy. Too many who seem to love this water also seem to have an already defeated attitude.

"This is hard to understand because if they would drink the water they could not help but to believe and be strong. I am afraid that they have only occasionally tasted it, but do not really drink from it. Their love is more for the idea of it than the reality. It is almost as if it is some kind of romantic fantasy to them, not reality."

"Do you know of any of the wells nearby?" I asked. "At the wells we must find some who are really drinking and may be willing to join us in this fight for the river."

"I know of a couple of wells not far from this valley. The water there is good, but not as good as this. Most of the wells have been too shallow to last for very long. They also get muddy fast. The wells do help some people, but it is only when the water flows like this in the open that it can turn a valley into a paradise like you see here. And this water must flow to stay alive and pure for very long."

I then heard footsteps behind me. I turned to see a man approaching.

4

THE PLAN

AS I WATCHED THE MAN APPROACH, IT SEEMED that he was dressed in the style of Colonial times. His hair was long and gray and I suspected it was a Colonial wig. He walked with purpose, and was a little bowlegged as if he had spent much of his life on a horse.

"She is right. Wells can help a few people, but they are mostly temporary. They often become polluted or dry up. You certainly have a treasure here," he remarked.

"Yes, I have never tasted anything so wonderful," I replied.

"I was talking about the girl," he said.

"Yes, she is truly remarkable for one so young. I have never met anyone like her," I responded.

"You are about to meet many more like her, both boys and girls. They will be better fighters than most men in your times. You must be prepared for them."

"How do I prepare for them?" I asked.

"You must learn to ride this horse."

"Who are you?" I inquired.

"I am John Wesley. I am speaking to you as a torchbearer who was also given a horse like this one. You are here to help prepare the coming ones. In my time there were but a handful of torchbearers and only a couple who rode the white horses. In your time there will be thousands of torchbearers and hundreds of these great stallions.

"You are here to learn about your purpose. You are called as one of those who will help awaken a coming great host. Then you must help to train them, preparing them for the last battle."

"I hardly feel that I can train anyone here. I am learning more from this little girl than I am teaching her," I responded sincerely.

"It is because you are willing to learn from her that you will become a trusted teacher. Keep drinking and keep listening. I will help you as will all of the torchbearers who have gone before you. I can teach you in a few hours what it took me a lifetime to learn. What we cannot give you the children will. They are wise because they are teachable.

"If you remain teachable, you will be wise beyond your years, regardless of how old you get to be. You can receive the wisdom of the ages. Remember that your primary purpose is to learn, not teach. The primary teaching that you have for the coming ones is to teach them how to learn. This is what it means to be a disciple— you are forever a student. Each one that you meet will teach you more about how to learn and you will teach them the same."

"We are certainly in a situation that is beyond my present knowledge or wisdom to know how to handle," I responded. "It seems that this horse and learning how to ride it are the keys to us defending this stream. If you are here to help me, I am ready."

"One thing that you must know and not forget," Wesley said sternly, "is that she is right when she said you cannot retreat. You are now surrounded and there is nowhere to run. There are a few wells left in this region, but they are drying up fast. You must defend this river and gather your army here."

"How do I gather an army if there are just a few wells in this region? Are there enough faithful ones to build an army?"

"No, there are not. You may gather a few from them, but your army is the very one that is descending on you here. Your victory over this evil horde is to convert its soldiers. Then you must teach them to drink from this stream. You must add to them others and they must go forth to conquer. I can also assure you that if you will fight and not give up, you cannot lose."

Then the little girl spoke up. "I knew it! Many of my friends and relatives are in that evil army. I knew they would one day be soldiers of the King."

"You are right," Wesley continued. "You must do more than just set them free from the bondage they are in. You must train, equip, and release them to go and recover the wells that the enemy has stopped up and heal the streams that have been polluted and buried."

As I looked up and thought about the huge horde above us, I remembered what a great general once said when he was told that he was surrounded, "Great! Now we have them where we want them— they can't get away this time! Attack in every direction!"

As I was thinking about this, I noticed Wesley looking at me, "Can you be so bold?"

"It doesn't seem that we have a choice," I replied. "It is a remarkable thing. They are so numerous and have us surrounded, and we are so few, and they are in our trap! Certainly, only the Lord could ever pull off such a victory."

"And certainly it will be the Lord who gets the credit for it," Wesley and the girl both said.

I looked at the fortress that the evil horde was building in the valley. Already it would be hard to conquer with many soldiers. I listened to the commotion of the horde that was at the top of the valley all around. It was massive, multitudes and multitudes. What could a girl, a horse, even John Wesley, and I do against such a force?

"I can no longer fight the battles which are on the earth. I am now a part of the great company of witnesses. Through my life I can still speak and teach, but you must do the fighting. I can encourage you that several times in my life I was surrounded like this, with very few with me. Each time I saw the victory of the Lord. Do not become discouraged by how dark it becomes or how many rise up against you. You cannot lose if you do not retreat."

Then the little girl chimed in, "I know my mother is a captive in the division called 'Ridicule.' She is there because she needs the approval of others. I also know that she has never known true love in her life. I know that if I can love her faithfully she will be freed.

"I believe all who are in that division are like her. We can free the captives with the truth of God's love. If we can do this with them, then there must be other keys that will set the captives in the other divisions free."

Wesley did not say anything but just looked at me to be sure that I understood how true this was. It was obvious that this simple truth was the key to our victory. The truth of who God is can break any bonds.

I then had to ask, "Please tell me, why are some given a torch but not a horse? How can we use them together, other than just being able to cover more ground?"

"Many have the honor of carrying a manifestation of the Lord's presence, but few are called to start a movement. The torches are all given to start movements, but not many carry them forward in such a way to start an advance of the truth. The horse represents the movement which you have been called to start.

"Movements have a purpose to take ground back from the enemy. They are for establishing strongholds of truth, which the enemy cannot prevail against. These become safe places for the captives who are released from their bondage to be healed, restored, and armed to go back out into the battle. Many will draw close to those who have the torch, but they will only follow into battle those who have the horse as well.

"Your first mission is to defend this place, and then mobilize those who are true seekers of the water of life. Then they must be trained and equipped to go and retake what that evil horde has fouled and trampled under its feet.

"Every captive which is freed from that horde can heal and restore more than they once destroyed. Life is stronger than death. Remember that you are not called to just take back the earth, but to restore those who are called to rule over the earth.

"As your armor bearer here has told you, the more who drink from this stream, the larger it will grow. In this way you can turn this little stream into a river that overflows until it reaches many other places. As it begins to grow here, when it breaks out in other valleys and deserts it will be much stronger and deeper."

"How do I draw others here?" I asked. "It is obvious that we need a lot of help if we are to convert this army that surrounds us."

"You will draw others by drinking from the river yourself. Remember that the river grows as you and others begin to drink from it. The blind will follow anyone who can see and the better you can see the more who will be drawn to you. When they come many will still be blind and most will be wounded.

"You must teach each one to drink until they are healed and can see. Regardless of what they look like at first, many who come to you will be the mighty ones that Enoch prophesied would come in your times."

Then he looked at me with a penetrating stare as if looking to see if I could understand something very important.

"The torch that you carry will also draw many to it, but the presence of the Lord is not enough."

"How could the presence of the Lord not be enough?" I asked. "There is nothing greater than that! It is even more wonderful and invigorating than this water," I protested.

"You are right about that, but many who love His presence still remain weak and immature because they only want to experience the joy of the Lord. Such are seldom willing to face the conflict of the times. His presence will always be the best and the most wonderful gift. Even so, for eternity we will have this. Right now there is a battle to be fought."

Wesley walked over to the little girl and laid his hands on her shoulders. Then he looked up at me and continued.

"You need worshipers who are also warriors. All who are not trained and equipped for the battle will be overcome by it. Even if they do love His presence, they must also be taught to love truth and to love it enough to resist the evil one. This is a strength that I developed to train and equip people to stand for truth and fight for it. That is why there are things you must learn from me.

"Few have been able to build the people into a force that conquers. I did this by building small groups of people into small fortresses of truth. Some of these rose up to take their neighbors for the gospel. Others grew into mighty fortresses that took villages. A few took cities. Together we shaped the destiny of nations—even your nation."

I felt when he said the words "your nation" that it was in some strange way the valley we were standing in. As I pondered this and looked back at him, he had that unmistakable knowing look. Then he continued.

"Your nation still honors Paul Revere for waking up the people and calling them to the battle, but even more than that, heaven will honor those who wake up the people and call them to the battle, which must soon be fought.

"Just as the great messengers of the church age were all but seeds of the mighty ones of valor who are now about to be released on the earth, the enemy has been sowing his seeds too. You will have to fight every evil that has been released on the earth, and fight it in its full maturity.

"With this horse you must ride and warn the people about the invasion of their land. You can mobilize them to fight the good fight. You cannot retreat any further. There is nowhere else to go, but if you resist the enemy he will eventually flee. If you do not resist you are doomed."

The little girl was watching me intently. She stood erect, vigilant, and ready. Both Wesley and I were looking at her. I thought she must be like Joan of Arc. If there are even a few more like her I knew that these would certainly be marvelous times. Wesley continued.

"The Lord called a dozen men. He changed them and then they changed the world. In your time He is going to do the same with children. It is also the time of the lioness. Great are the company of women who will preach the gospel. There will be many great men of God in your time—but the great marvel, and the great honor, will be for the women and children who walk in the ways of the Lord.

"Remember, it was the woman who was deceived and would have enmity with the serpent, but it will be her seed that crushes its head. Women have a special place in this fight."

He looked into the eyes of the little girl. "It is your time as a woman. It is your time as a child, for the children will be for signs and wonders. They will turn the tide of the last battle. Gather the children and help their mothers. Great is the Lord in you for all that you need."

My attention was then caught by something flickering out of the corner of my eye. The fortress that the evil ones had built was being used to hurl fiery arrows in all directions. It was apparent that they were trying to scorch the beautiful valley that we were in.

Wesley turned and put both hands on my shoulders just as the Lord had done, saying, "You can't put out every little fire. You must destroy that fortress."

Then I was suddenly alone and sitting in my room.

5

THE SWORD

I SAT IN MY HOTEL ROOM WONDERING if it had all been a dream, a vision, or if it had really happened. I wanted to quickly write everything down so I would not forget it, but I was exhausted. I decided to lie down on the bed for a few minutes to rest.

Immediately I was suspended in a brilliant blue sky. As a pilot I used to say that my office was the sky, and had always deeply cherished the time that I spent there, but I had never seen a sky as beautiful as this. I felt more at home than I ever had before.

Then I felt earth under my feet. I was again on a seashore. I knew I was in the heavenly realm again by the air that I was breathing and the breathtaking beauty of all that I saw.

As I looked, I felt that this was the earth as it was meant to be. The desire grew within me to take this beauty and this air to the earth somehow. As much as I loved just standing in that place, I knew I had to leave soon, that I had to go back. There was a deep compulsion growing in me to make the earth right again.

Then I felt the presence of the Lord behind me, but when I turned to see Him, He was not there. I closed my eyes to just focus on breathing the air. When I opened my eyes, I was standing in yet another place.

I was in the middle of a street, alone. I did not recognize it, but I knew it was a street in London. The peace I had felt in the heavenly place was still with me, but fading fast as I looked at my surroundings.

The torch was in my hand, but as my peace faded, the torch became heavier. I knew that I had to focus on the Lord and sense His presence again. As I did, the peace returned somewhat, and the torch became a little lighter. I began to feel great danger. I determined to keep my peace, and even though I was not afraid, I was more vigilant.

I determined to keep my main attention on the torch while glancing periodically at my surroundings. I saw no threat but continued to feel danger. Down the middle of the street there was a grass strip that was about fifteen meters wide. It had trees down the center that were surrounded by little protective metal fences.

I began to walk down the street. Then I noticed one little fence that did not have a tree near it. I just assumed the tree that had been there had died. This did not seem like a big deal at first, but I began to feel grief for the missing tree that I could not shake. I stopped beside the empty fence to ponder what I was feeling. When I did this, I felt the Lord standing behind me.

"Put the torch there," He said.

I walked over and placed the torch in the middle of the little fence, gently pushing it into the ground so that it stood up straight. It was quickly planted firmly as if it had sunk deep roots into the ground. I reached out to see if I could pick it up, and I could very easily, even though there were already long roots attached to it. I put it back and watched. It was strongly rooted again, and the fire did not dim.

"You were able to pick it up easily because you have the authority," a voice behind me said.

I turned around to see who had spoken and saw a man who appeared to be a street person, or homeless man. He was standing beside a stairway to a house.

"Pardon me," I said, "But how do you know about this torch?"

He did not answer my question but just continued his statement, "Each of these trees was once a torch and carried by someone like you. This is a city where movements become monuments."

I did not like the sound of that at all. My torch was still alive, and I did not want it to just become a tree lining an obscure street. I wanted to pick it up and take it with me, but then the Lord had told me to place it there. I did not know what to do. Obviously seeing my dilemma the man continued.

"Before the end comes, there will be movements that do not stop moving. Maybe you are one of those who can carry such a movement. Even so, for now you must do as the Lord told you and leave the torch where it is. I perceive that you are not yet ready to carry it very far, much less carry it to the end."

"Who are you?" I asked.

"I am a watcher," he said, and with that he vanished.

I then looked at the street again to try to recognize it. I wanted to know the name of the street, and where it was located in the city. I knew I was in a vision, but I felt like this was a real street in London as well. I wanted to find it when I came out of the vision. I felt that it was an avenue of monuments though I could not see any monuments from where I was standing.

I turned around to touch the torch so that its fire could surge through me. I needed more clarity. As I did, I was suddenly in yet another place, standing in front of the Lord. He was holding a large sword. The blade was brilliant, made of something that looked like silver, but it was almost transparent. It flashed with brilliant colors like a diamond. The thought came to me that silver would not make a very strong blade, and as the Lord often did, He answered my thoughts.

"This is silver, but it is stronger than any metal. This sword is a divinely powerful weapon. It is the power of My redemption. The one who carries it must be in unity with My redemptive purposes. You must have a heart to redeem or it will become too heavy for you to carry. You must be able to carry this too if you are to carry the torch very far."

I continued to look at the sword. It was of a very plain design and it did not just reflect light—it emitted light. The light coming from it was of many different colors, like light that has passed through a prism. The glory of the light that came from it made it the most beautiful sword I had ever seen even though the design was so plain. It was as captivating as the torch.

The Lord took the sword by the blade and extended the handle to me so I could take it. I thought it would be very heavy because of its size, but it seemed to not weigh more than an ounce or two.

"It will only become heavy if you try to wield it in your own strength. This is My Word of redemption. It cannot be destroyed, but will stand forever. This is from My armory. This is the weapon that will be carried by My prophets in the last days.

"No power on the earth is stronger than My redemption. However, if you use it wrongly, it can bring great troubles to the earth. With this sword those that you bless will be blessed. If you bless a devil, it will be blessed and will prosper. You must be careful not to try to redeem that which My Father did not plant, but you must go forth to redeem."

As I looked at the handle I noticed five brilliant gems. One was blue, one green, another one was clear like a diamond, one was red, and one was amber. The handle itself was plain, but the beauty of the seemingly transparent gold was stunning. It was the most beautiful sword I had ever seen, not because of its design, but because of what it was made of. Even so, it was obviously not made for show. I knew even the gems were there for a functional purpose, but I was not sure yet what it was.

I raised the sword and waved it in the air. My arm did not get tired at all, but rather the opposite—the waving of it gave me strength. As strength came into my arm, it continued on through my whole body. When I felt it reach my eyes, everything became brighter, more clear. As I continued to wave the sword, I could see farther.

I then looked at the sword again. As I looked, my eyes began to magnify it like a powerful magnifying glass. I could see that the sword was also alive. Even the gems were alive!

"The Spirit moved in the beginning," the Lord continued. "The Spirit never stops moving. This is the sword of the Spirit. As it is moving, strength is released to the one who bears it. It will quicken your mortal body.

"Remember that My Word is never still, but living, sharp, and active. Remember that life always moves. That is why My work on the earth is often called 'a movement.' Just as I created the universe to ever expand, My Word will be forever moving and expanding. Those who know the life that is in Me will also forever be expanding in knowledge, wisdom, and power. They will never stop growing.

"As long as you abide in Me, you will forever be growing in both knowledge and power. I now give you the command to move and grow. In due time I will give you the command to multiply and conquer, not by taking lives, but by saving them."

As always when the Lord spoke, I wanted to memorize every word. I felt the life coming through them was like that which came by waving the sword. As I considered what He had said, my love for the sword grew.

I could not believe such a gift was possible. I wanted to hold it forever. What it imparted to me was different from the torch, but was just as wonderful. It strengthened me and gave me courage. I knew that together the sword and the torch would give me a clarity of perception that was greater than anything I had yet experienced. Even as I was thinking this, I could tell that I was not only getting stronger, but healthier. I felt toxins in me being washed away.

Then I began to feel a deep passion in my heart for this sword. I wanted it to touch everyone that I loved. I knew if it touched those I did not love that I would begin to love them.

"What you are feeling is the passion for My Word. You are holding My living Word. This is what the true love of My Word does. Those who have the true love of My truth love those for whom I gave it. The Spirit is again going to breathe on the Scriptures. This love for My Word will come upon My messengers in your time," the Lord said very soberly.

"What a treasure," I continued to think. "How could anyone not love this?" I wondered. I badly wanted to start using the sword. Then I felt a strong compulsion to use it on myself—to plunge it deep into my own heart.

"Do it," the Lord said.

I pointed its blade at my heart and thrust it into my chest. As I did, it disappeared as if it had been absorbed into me. There was just a slight tinge of pain, but when I looked there was no wound. Then the sense of strength that I had felt it imparting to me grew much faster.

In just a few moments, I felt as if I could fly, lift buildings, and even walk through walls. I began to feel that I could do anything because the power within me was so great that I did not have to obey the physical laws. I also felt there was no limit to how far I could see, or how much I could magnify anything that I looked upon to see it in more detail.

My mind then began to awaken. Understanding began to grow within me until I felt like the universe was opened before me, perceiving and understanding its secrets. This was another kind of incredibly wonderful feeling.

I was seeing everything by the Spirit, not just through my own eyes and mind. I felt at one with everything that I looked upon. I also felt great love for everything that I looked upon. There was no earthly feeling that could compare to this and it was growing.

"That is the power of My Word for those who will receive it into their heart," the Lord explained. "To receive My Word into your heart must be your quest every day. Then you will begin to see. Then you will have understanding.

"It was by My Word that the universe was created and it is by My Word that it is held together. My Word is the answer to every human problem. If you will receive My Word into your heart, it will grow within you and you will never stop growing.

"Your mind will continue to open and your knowledge will forever grow. I created the mind of man to ever expand so that you could know Me, My ways, and My works.

"You must receive My Word into your heart first, then it will open your mind. If you only receive it into your mind, it will not live. My living Word must be received into your heart first and then your mind will open."

I could not help but to think of the ancient controversy, "Does one need to understand in order to believe, or must we believe in order to understand?" I knew the answer.

"You are right," He said. "Only when you believe can you understand. Even so, it is right to seek understanding. When your understanding ceases to grow, you have departed from the path of life. As long as you are on that path you will grow. Your understanding will grow as well."

As the Lord spoke, I turned to look at Him. I began to see glory that was beyond any human language to describe. I physically felt the glory that I was seeing. I knew it was because the Lord and the sword that I had plunged into my heart were one. When His Word was in my heart, I was able to see His glory as never before.

As I looked at Him, my vision continued to grow. As it grew, I saw more and more of His glory. I knew this could be never ending and I never wanted it to end. I understood how the cherubim and angelic majesties who had worshiped before Him for ages and ages were in a continual state of such awe and wonder that they never wanted to do anything else. I wanted to stand there forever and join them.

"This is a taste of the joy that is in true life," the Lord continued. "True life is only found in Me. This joy is your strength. For those who follow Me this joy will not only be theirs forever—it will grow forever.

"Now you must remember this. The joy of My presence can alone sustain you through what is coming upon the earth. You will know My joy and it will increase in you, but to do My work on the earth you must also know My sorrow."

Then He turned around and I saw His back. He was still wounded and the wounds were terrible. As I looked at them, they were magnified. I began to see darkness, disease, despair, and death. I felt grief and mourning that was worse than anything I had ever felt before. The grief grew to be as strong as the joy had been. I felt that I was gazing into hell itself.

As I continued looking, I saw anger cascading into rage and murder until blood flowed like a river. I saw lust grow into a raging, hot disease that was erupting like a volcano, destroying everything in its path.

Over everything I felt a gripping selfishness, which was the exact opposite of the oneness with everything that I had felt before, and it released a choking darkness that burned my lungs. It too was growing and expanding. When I felt I could not live much longer in the terror and despair that I was feeling, I cried out for the Lord to save me or kill me.

The Lord turned around. My strength had left me. I collapsed to the ground still wanting to die. Lying there I could hear Him, but He seemed to be very far away. I had seemingly lost all comprehension of the glory that I had seen just moments before. "Could the darkness be that much stronger than the glory?" I wondered.

"That was a taste of the power that you are facing in your times. If you had not first tasted of My glory, you would not have lived. I have overcome all evil and you will come to know the power of My glory over all evil, but you must know the power of the evil that men on the earth are about to face. You must learn to walk in My presence in the midst of evil and prevail. If you do not abide in Me, you will be overcome."

I heard everything the Lord said, though He still seemed far away. I then felt something in my hand. It was the sword. It was moving back and forth on its own. It gripped my hand rather than me gripping it. Soon strength began to return to me.

Slowly I got up. I felt filthier than I could ever remember feeling. Gradually, the feeling began to fade as if I was being washed by the gentle breeze, which the waving sword was creating. Soon I was able to stand. Then I could see the Lord and His glory again.

"What you saw is the burden that I carry," the Lord said. "You saw what is now happening on the earth. The darkness is growing too. The earth itself will not be able to bear the evil of man much longer. The earth itself will rebel against man and terror will increase as the earth begins to rage and travail.

"Man is about to know fear such as has not been known since the beginning. Those who abide in Me will likewise rise in faith as has never been demonstrated on the earth before. Because of the fear which is now being released, I have reserved the greatest demonstrations of faith for this time."

"Lord, how can anyone survive?" I begged, still feeling a little shaken from what I had seen. "The darkness even seemed to overcome the glory and beauty that I was beholding."

"The time is approaching when no man can survive what they have released upon themselves and they would all perish if I did not put an end to it. I have redeemed the earth. In the greatest darkness I will release an even greater light. The greater light is My love for the world and My redemption.

"You must learn to carry the torch and the sword into the darkness. You must learn to carry My love and My redemption at all times. When you learn to love the most wretched and most worthless, even those who are in the grips of the deep darkness, then My Word of redemption is truly established in your heart. The power of My redemption will then flow through you.

"When Moses asked to see My glory, I showed him My back. He saw the stripes that I was to take for the sins of the world and he saw what you saw, which is what I bore at the cross, the sin that I have already paid for. That is My glory too.

"It is right for you to want to see My face, to know the beauty and life that is in Me. It is right for you to want to carry that to the world, but there is another glory which you must know and carry. This is the pain that I bore for you.

"The world's greatest heroes are those who overcome the greatest enemies. The greatest saints are those who overcome the greatest darkness. You are being sent to call those who will serve Me in the darkest of times. Therefore, you must know the depths of My redemption.

"You must know in the depths of your heart My love for those who are in the grip of the greatest evil. You must also know that the power of My redemption is great enough even for them. The sword that is being given to My messengers in the last days can break any yoke and cut through any chain. My light is stronger than any darkness."

His words washed over me so that I continued to feel a deep cleansing from all I had seen of the darkness. As I listened, I continued to wave the sword until I felt my vision and strength completely return. I knew that I could not forget the power of the Word of redemption to cleanse my soul and restore my vision and strength.

My heart was warming and I knew it was the life of the sword that had been thrust into it, as well as its power in my hand. I knew this connection between the Word in my heart and my hand was the connection between faith and works. It took both to cleanse and restore me just as it does everyone. This was the understanding that I could never forget. After a time the Lord continued:

"You must have the sword and the torch. You must live in My manifest presence, and you must have My Word in your heart and your hand. You must teach this to My messengers. No one will make it through the times ahead without both. You must grow in the light faster than the darkness is growing. My light is stronger, but to remain light it must be growing."

As I listened, I instinctively continued waving the sword and the strength continued to increase. Again I began to feel that I could fly— that I could overcome any earthly power. As I continued looking at the Lord, His glory was growing and expanding.

I then grasped the sword with both hands as tightly as I could. I knew what was coming, and I knew what I had to do. The Lord turned around again so that I could see His back. When He did, I stepped into the darkness.

6

THE POWER

I WAS ONCE AGAIN ON THE AVENUE where I had placed the torch. I then realized that I had entered into the darkness without taking the torch with me, but had somehow returned to the street where I had left it. I could not see the torch from where I was so I began to walk, waving the sword as I did. I knew I had to find the torch.

As I walked, I started to feel increasing darkness and oppression. It was indeed an avenue of monuments. As I waved the sword and my vision grew, I became alarmed that there did not seem to be life anywhere. The trees and grass in the middle of the street were green, but I did not feel life in them. I suspected that they were artificial, but when I looked more closely they had all of the functions of life but were dead somehow.

I continued to walk. It was a cold, damp, and dreary place. Finally, I came to a monument. It was the green and brown of tarnished bronze which seemed to increase the dreariness of this place. The statue was fastened to a marble foundation, but it all felt cold and meaningless. Even so, I felt that it was the statue of a great person, though I did not recognize who it was.

I continued on, gently swinging the sword, not knowing what else to do. Then I saw a golden glow in the distance. It appeared to be life. As I approached it, I saw that it was a tree. It was still rather small, hardly taller than I was, but I was astonished by what I saw as I stepped up to it.

The tree was the torch that I had left. It had grown and now had branches. It was full of life. It stood out in this place like an oasis in a desert. I reached out to grasp the branch closest to me. Immediately, it fell into my hand. It was a torch just like the first one, which was now a tree.

"Take it back to the monument," a voice behind me said.

I turned to see a white eagle. He was whiter than I had remembered him, having seen him before, but I thought it must be because of the darkness of the place we were in. I also knew that he had become even wiser. His talons stood out sharper and more powerful and his eyes were more piercing.

"You were right to plant the torch. If you had held onto it, you would have had one good torch, but now you will have many."

"How is that?" I asked. "And where are we?"

"You are in the heart of a great city that has died but is about to live again."

"Is this where you're from?" I asked, knowing that it wasn't, but just wanting to keep the conversation going until I thought of something better to say.

"I have friends here and a few disciples. They will help you with what you are here to do."

"What is that?"

"You have the torch and the sword and you are here, so you are going to use them here."

"I hardly know how to use them. They were just given to me." Sensing a bit of impatience rise in the eagle I continued, "But I will do the best I can. Tell me what you know about my purpose here."

"That's my job and I will tell you all that I can. I'm also glad to hear that you do not know too much. You're safer that way. You will know what to do when it is time to do it. My young friends will help you."

"Where will you be?"

"I will be watching, just as I was when you touched the sea with the torch a few years ago."

"A few years ago—it could not have been more than a couple of hours ago!" I protested.

"No, it was over five years ago. Remember that time in the heavenly realm does not seem the same as on the earth. I saw you when you did it. From the time the Lord gave you the torch until you touched the water with it was three years, so He gave it to you eight years ago."

"I don't remember you being there. Where were you?"

"Remember, I don't have to be there to see. I also saw the other gifts you received, and those that you will soon be given. It is time for them, but there are still many things for you to learn. Your training is not over, but the time on earth is short. You must learn fast, but you must learn to teach others faster."

I looked down at the sword and torch that were in my hands. I looked around and wanted to use them both, but did not know what to do with them. So I just held onto the torch and waved the sword.

"I am here to help you get started," the old eagle said, "Others will help you along the way. Now, go back to the monument you passed, and touch it with the torch and watch."

The old eagle spread his wings and he lifted high into the dark sky on a wind that I could not feel. Even though he soon disappeared,

I could feel him and knew that he was watching. I then began to feel many others watching me as well.

I started to walk, holding the torch out in front, waving the sword as I went. I felt increasing strength and my vision grew. As this happened I wanted to attack the darkness. "I was born for this," I thought to myself.

"Yes you were," an unfamiliar voice answered. "You and many others, too. This is your time."

Turning I saw another eagle, much younger than the first. Even so, this young one seemed even more regal than the older one. It was the way he thrust his chest out a little more while his wings were slightly open as if ready to soar at any moment. It was obvious that he had explosive energy, but contained it with great grace. As if he heard every thought, he responded:

"I am of another generation. I am not greater than my father, but I have been given more authority. I am here to awaken and guide the great champions who are now maturing on the earth. I will help you and the others who are to prepare them for what is to come."

"How will I prepare them?"

"First you will learn to use the sword and the torch for more than just edifying yourself. That is important to know, but it is just the beginning. When you have used what is in your hand, you will begin to understand the rest of what you are to be given. Then you will know what you are to do with all of your gifts."

We began to walk. My eyes turned toward the trees that we were passing. I then noticed the fruit. It was beautiful, compelling, and I felt a tinge of hunger.

"Don't even look at it," the young eagle stated as if he had to repeat this often.

"Why?" I asked. "It looks like very good fruit and I am very hungry." Then I sensed why I could not eat from them. "These are all trees of the knowledge of good and evil, aren't they?"

"They are. How did you know?"

"They seem to be alive, but they're dead and the fruit looks delicious. Why is it they are on this avenue of monuments? And why is it full of these trees?"

"The monuments are to people who were alive, but are now dead. These monuments are to people who were given life to give to the earth, but after beginning in the Spirit, they tried to complete the work by their own wisdom and ways. By that they began to cultivate these trees. That is why they exist together on this road.

"This is one of the main avenues that the people of this city come to. They do not love these monuments, but the monuments make them feel secure and significant as if they were the heirs of the greatness of those represented. They also love the fruit from these trees, even though it is poison to them and it kills them just as it killed their empire."

As we walked, my vision continued to increase. I began to see that the street was very wide, well manicured, and would have been very beautiful in sunlight. It still felt dead. The young eagle soared above me and I knew he was watching me closely and discerning my thoughts.

"What am I going to do here with the sword and torch?" I asked him.

"First, understand these monuments. Even the smallest touch of life from God has the power to grow into that which would have restored the earth and made it a garden again. These monuments are to people that had life. They froze into dead monuments because they started thinking about how to build a monument to their own life. There is no purpose to building a monument on the earth! They will all perish!

"What you are to build is part of the heavenly city. You will fail in your purpose if you care what men think of your work. You must only care what the Lord thinks of it. You are not here to build monuments, but a movement that will not stop moving. The River of Life never stops moving. The Spirit never stops moving. If you stop, you will have departed from the way of the Spirit and the way of life."

As we approached the monument that I had passed earlier, the young eagle stopped and said, "You must bring this monument to life again."

"Why would we want to do that?" I protested. "And how?"

"The Father loves redemption. The King loves redemption. He also honors the fathers who walked in His ways upon the earth, even if they only walked in them for a little while. These monuments were not His will, but He is going to redeem them and use them for the sake of the fathers and for the sake of their children who now live in this city.

"Remember, Ishmael was not His will either. Even so, He blessed Ishmael and made him a great nation. You will be surprised by how the sons of Ishmael will glorify the Lord at the end. You will also be surprised by how these monuments will as well.

"If you want to stay on the path of life, you must love redemption the way He does. It is a part of your purpose to help redeem monuments. That is why you are here with the sword and the torch."

"But I thought they fell by building these to themselves," I protested again. "How am I going to help redeem them? What will either the sword or torch do for these dead monuments?"

"You will continue to walk in darkness if your understanding of redemption does not grow. You must honor these fathers and mothers. You must touch them with the word and with the fire. When you do, the life that was in them which is eternal, will flow from them again. You cannot attain to your own destiny without the life that they had.

"The Lord is going to make these monuments live and living water will flow from them again. This will be a token of His redemption power and His resurrection. These trees look alive but are dead and their fruit is death. These monuments look dead but they still have life in them. The life that they carried is eternal. Put the torch to that statue."

I lifted the torch and put it under the face of what was a great English poet's statue. Quickly it renewed the bronze so that it began to shine. Soon the whole face was glowing.

"That is enough," the eagle said.

I backed up and watched. The statue was still a statue, but there was life in the face just as there was life in the torch and sword that I held. I then took the sword and plunged it into the heart of the statue. It went in easily all the way to the hilt.

As I drew it out, the breast of the statue began to burn with the glow of the sunset/sunrise colors and of the torch. As this happened there was also a slight glow on the horizon. I was again astonished by the wonders of the torch and sword—how they did not take life but gave it.

"They can kill too," said the eagle which was now soaring above me. "They bring life back to that which had life, but the great danger is they can also give life to that which was dead."

"What do you mean?" I asked.

"You have the power of blessing in your hands. What you bless will be blessed even if it is not what the Lord wants to be blessed. If you bless the work of the enemy, it will prosper. You must only bless by the command of the Lord.

"The enemy only receives his authority on earth from man, and the greater the authority that you have been entrusted with, the greater the harm you can do when you use it wrongly, and the greater the enemy is empowered when you give it to him.

"You have great blessing or great destruction in your hands. You must only build what the Lord wants built and tear down that which the Lord wants you to tear down. You have been given both tools and weapons. The more powerful they become in your hands, the more careful you must be."

"Well, I think I should begin to kill those trees," I replied.

"Yes, that you will do at the proper time, but now is not the time. For now we will concentrate on giving life. These trees are still useful to the Lord."

"How is that?"

"The Lord put The Tree of the Knowledge of Good and Evil in the center of the Garden of Eden for a crucial reason. There can be no obedience from the heart unless there is the freedom to disobey. These trees attract people to this place. Some who come because of the trees will notice that there is life again in our friend here.

"When anyone touches him that life will grow. Life grows with interaction. We do not know if his message will be completely restored, but it is possible. His teaching could begin to flow through the earth again. But that is not in our hands. You have done your part, so now we must move on."

"Where are we going?"

"There are other monuments in this city that you must touch and help to bring back to life. If the people respond to them, streams of living water will begin to flow throughout this city. Then they will join to form a great river. If enough are awakened to those who lived in their past, there will be life in the present, and they will flow together down the great river that will carry them to a glorious future."

"If you are an eagle here, you must have seen into the future of this city. Will that happen here again?" I asked, not wanting to waste time with monuments if it did not produce results.

"It is not our place to be concerned with results. The Lord gives everyone a chance, even when He knows they will reject it. However, when I fly high enough I can see into the future, but only a narrow part of it. I know that life will flow through this city again, and I know that so many of my kind would not be here if the potential of this city were not great.

"It is our place to use the gifts that we have been given and trust the Lord with the results. You must learn well the lessons of this city. You will then be sent to many cities and nations to do it again. You are called to give life to cities and nations by giving life to their past, their monuments. There are others doing the same, and there are others who are preparing for the harvest in other ways, but this is your part."

As I walked and the eagle continued to soar above me, I felt an urge to strike one of the trees of knowledge with my sword just to see what would happen.

"Go ahead," the now faint voice above me encouraged.

I struck the tree just above the little fence at its base. The sword easily passed through it. I watched to see if it would fall over, but it did not. Then the fruit began to fall from it. Soon it gave off a terrible stench. I looked at the fruit still on the tree and it was rotting right before my eyes. I backed far enough away so that none of it would fall on me.

"That's how the Lord cursed the fig tree," I heard the eagle say from above, also marveling at the sight. "That sword is His Word. It can give life or it can take it."

I then stepped close enough to put the torch to the side of the tree. The fire took to the tree as if it was dry paper, consuming it quickly. There was nothing left but ashes. Then a breeze came and blew the ashes away. Soon there was no evidence that the tree had even been there.

"Those *are* divinely powerful weapons!" the eagle remarked. "That tree has deceived many people."

"That was fast," I responded. "I can't believe it happened so fast."

"I wouldn't call seventeen years *fast*," the old eagle retorted, having appeared seemingly out of nowhere. He was obviously irritated.

"You have both been very foolish! Remember that time is not the same here. That is why on the earth patience must be joined to your faith or you will miss the timing of the Lord. We will have to return to clean up this mess," he said, departing as fast as he had come. He seemed to be in a terrible hurry.

I still did not know why the old eagle had been so irritated. I could also tell that my young eagle friend was likewise confused. I was sorry that he had not explained it to us. I began to walk again and touch more monuments. Soon I could tell that the day was dawning. It was not as dreary either. I knew the sun would soon break through the fog.

"Many thought that this city had no future, that its night had come for good, but its greatest day may just be starting," I said to the young eagle who was still with me.

I could feel a great hope rising in me for the city. I then noticed that he did not seem to hear. He was trying to look far away into the future.

I too became lost in my own thoughts. I began to think of the valley, the horse, and the little girl. I wondered if Rivers of Life were about to begin in this city again. I wondered if there was a connection so that they could flow into that valley also.

I became deeply concerned for that brave little girl. Her grace, wisdom, and maturity so far beyond her years made her one of the greatest treasures I had ever found. I wanted to get back, but I knew that what I was being given here and what I was learning was part of the plan for her and the valley she was trying to defend.

I looked up again at the eagle. He had obviously seen something, but I could not tell if he was rejoicing or alarmed. As I looked up at him, I soon began to feel what he felt. I knew that my training was almost over. The alarm was about to be sounded. A great battle was about to begin.

7

THE QUEEN

THE YOUNG EAGLE LANDED BESIDE ME.

"I know what you are about to tell me," I said.

The young eagle looked at me with raised eyebrows and then continued with what he had started to say.

"Things are happening faster than I thought. For the first time I did not want to fly higher so I could see farther. I was not ready to see what I did. I must gather the other eagles and find our father. The future is very dark. Keep going and I will see you again soon."

He was off before I could protest. I was sorry I had been so quick to speak, implying I already knew what he was about to say. I knew his news was bad, but I did not know the details.

"My stupid pride," I thought. I resolved to never do that again. It always seemed to cost me knowledge. I walked on, waving the sword and holding the torch as close as I could, wondering what the young eagle had seen.

I then came upon the statue of a lady. She was astonishingly beautiful and I presumed that she had been an English queen. As I looked at her closely, my heart almost stopped. Not only did I know her face very well, but she was alive and pointing her scepter straight at me.

Eagles sat on her and were all around her base like pigeons usually are around statues. They too were all looking at me. When she spoke it was with a dignity I knew very well and she had an authority which made me tremble.

"You're the little girl I left in the valley! How did you get here, and how is it that you are a monument?" I stammered. She did not answer, but looked at me curiously. One of the eagles then spoke.

"You forget that time here is not the same as in the earthly realm. However, this is not the girl you have seen, but she is a descendant of our lady."

I turned to the lady. "I'm sorry. I was just shocked when I saw you since you look so much alike."

The great lady seemed to disregard what I said and continued to hold her scepter out toward me as she began to speak.

"Will you awaken mothers to the glory of their calling? Will you give my daughters swords and torches? They are the ones who keep the torches alive and they will wield the sword wisely. My daughters will stop the death and bring back the life!"

I stood in speechless awe. Her words came with authority and nobility, which were as beautiful as she was. I did not want her to stop speaking because her words were so exhilarating.

"Are you Elizabeth?" I asked.

"No."

"Are you Mary, the mother of Jesus?"

Gazing at me with eyes that were warm, yet firm, it seemed that the faintest smile crossed her lips as she answered.

"You know me. Elizabeth knew me. Abraham searched for me. I am not Mary, but I too am a mother to Jesus. I am Jerusalem above. I am your mother too because I am the mother of all who worship in Spirit and truth."

As I looked at her I thought how she seemed to be motherhood in all of its glory. Her words did not just impart truth but life, hope, courage, and strength. It was impossible to consider that a woman could be more attractive, and yet there was not a hint of seduction or sexual attraction.

I just wanted to get as close to her as I could. Her presence was so warm and inviting that I began to move closer. I could not help but to marvel at how anyone who was such a light could be on this avenue of the monuments and not wake up the entire city.

"Why are you here? Why are you in this city?" I asked. "How could anyone with such grace and life be on this avenue? Why are there not multitudes sitting at your feet?"

"Men have made many monuments to me, but I have never died. Many have tried to bring me down to earth. They have mostly been those who have sat at my feet, trying to use me. They try to bring me to earth through their own works rather than faith, which alone can establish me on the earth.

"You can see me as you do now because of the vision that you have. If your vision were greater I would be even more to you. You are really only seeing a little more of me than those who only see a bronze statue.

"I do have some in this city who have begun to see me as more than just a statue. That is why I am alive here. As their vision grows I will be revealed more and more to this city.

"When they start to believe their vision in their hearts and not just their minds, I will be free from this avenue of monuments and will be raised above the palaces and castles of men. When that happens, the King will come to this city."

Then she looked at my hands and another faint smile creased her lips.

"You have the torch and sword. It is time for them here. No one can see me who does not honor the fathers and mothers. If you honor the fathers and mothers, you will give swords to the sons and daughters."

Her words were like fire and honey together. They burned, but they also sweetened and soothed. I could not imagine anyone not wanting to stay as close to her as they possibly could. She too could obviously hear my thoughts, and answered them.

"As I said, most only see me as a monument, cold and tarnished. When people begin to see me as I am they are drawn to me like a nursing child to its mother. I too have been made to be a desire of every searching heart. The King and I are one.

"You must remember this. It takes the light from both the fathers and mothers, sons and daughters, to reveal me as I am. I am much more than you are seeing now, and I am also as the child you met in the valley.

"No one can see me as I am if they do not see the glory of spiritual motherhood as well as fatherhood. It is because many honored only the fathers, but not the mothers too, that they and their fruit did not remain long on the earth. You must honor the fathers and mothers to bring forth the sons and daughters.

"No one can see me as I am who does not see the glory in the children. I have the wisdom of the ages and the wisdom of the new birth. It is the wisdom of the fathers and mothers, old and young, which the path of life follows."

As I listened I was drawn to the trees which lined the avenue. It did not escape her notice, and she again answered my thoughts.

"Yes, the woman was deceived and ate the forbidden fruit first. However, the man ate it even though he knew what he was doing. And, does the prophecy not say that the seed of the *woman* will crush the head of the serpent?"

"I'm sorry," I responded. "It's just that I have had so much teaching on how women are so easily deceived that I was actually wondering if anyone could think that way in your presence."

"I understand why many think this way, but you must now understand this—those who are redeemed are a new creation and are higher than the former creation. The new creation woman is higher than the former.

"When you become a part of the new creation, your weaknesses are transformed into strengths. Most of those who have the great gifts of discernment on the earth are women. Remember, in the new creation all things become new. That is why those with renewed minds do not judge after the flesh, but after the Spirit.

"The new creation woman is about to be revealed and all who see her will honor her. Neither my sons nor my daughters can see me as I am unless they begin to look at me together, opening their hearts to what each other sees. My sons *and* my daughters must prophesy. You must give torches and swords to my daughters as well as my sons, or you too will end up as just another statue on this street.

"You are concerned that the daughters are easily deceived. All may be deceived, but the wisdom of the women could keep you from much folly, like the folly of cutting down that tree!"

When she said this I shuddered. I knew immediately that something more terrible than I had imagined had happened.

"I just used my sword to cut down a tree which was bearing evil fruit. How could that have been bad? What kind of problems could that have created?" I asked.

"You did not plant a righteous tree in its place. Now it has sprouted again, and the power of evil within it has multiplied. You cannot just dispel the evil, but you must always fill its place with good or this will happen."

As much as I did not want to leave the presence of this great queen, I turned and began to run back to the place where I had cut down the tree. As I ran, I glanced back for one more look at her great beauty and I saw her motioning for the eagles to go with me. The deep concern on all of them was so obvious that I stopped.

"Tell me. How bad is it?" I cried out.

The great lady looked at me as if she were measuring the depths of my soul. I knew she was considering whether I could handle the answer. She must have concluded that I could not handle it because she said nothing. Then one of the eagles spoke up.

"You will understand very soon what has happened. We were not ready and I don't think you are ready for what is now upon us. Even so, we must go now. The battle for this city and many other cities has begun."

There was a knock at the door and I woke up with a start. The clock by the bed flashed 5:55. It was hard for me to get oriented.

I felt caught between two worlds. I continued looking at the clock and prayed for the grace to make it through what was coming. I knew there was indeed a bridge between the realms of heaven and earth and that what I had seen was very real.

I also thought about how the timing between them was not as it seemed. Sometimes minutes, or hours, in the heavenly realm turned out to be years on earth. Even so, I knew it was time to wake up. The last battle was really about to begin. Then I realized that there was no one at my bedroom door.

I had to sit for a while. I thought about how the "Jerusalem above" was worth searching for like no other treasure on earth. This is what the church is called to be. There is no question that if she is seen as she really is, the nations will come to her light! Who would not come to her?

How badly I wanted every church and believer to get just a glimpse of her—to hear her words, to feel the majesty of her presence, and the dignity of her every move! She was womanhood in all of its glory. She is a bride worthy of the King!

I was consumed with searching for a way to share what I had seen. I wanted desperately to tell all believers what they were called to be a part of, but my words were too inadequate.

"She does not belong in the avenue of monuments. She belongs on the highest hill so that all can see her!" I thought, but my words seemed as dry and dead as the other monuments. I began to long for the words of life.

Then I began to think of the impending battle. A dread came over me like a dark blanket. My strength left me. I was so weary I easily drifted off to sleep.

Then I saw her again. She was no longer a statue on the avenue of monuments—she was a warrior clothed in brilliant armor. She was more regal than human words can describe. Her presence exuded grace and strength, which filled me with awe. She looked me right in the eyes as a most genuine and brilliant smile crossed her lips.

"Do not fear. I too was brought to earth for the battle that is now upon us. I must be known as motherhood itself, but I must also be known as a warrior too. Do not fear. The light that is in us is greater than the darkness. It is time for the light to be seen, and it is time fight."

8

THE TREE AND ITS FRUIT

I WAS RUNNING AS FAST AS I COULD toward the place where I had cut down the tree with my sword. I knew something terrible had happened, but I could not understand what it was.

Then I began to smell a terrible stench, like rotting fruit, but far more pungent than any I had ever smelled. It was then that I saw it—a tree that towered over all of the others. It reached such a height that it covered a large section of the avenue of the monuments. Its leafy boughs were so thick that it was dark beneath it.

As I proceeded toward it, I began to hear crashing noises which became louder as I moved closer. I slowed down as every sense within was telling me that this was more ominous than anything I had ever faced.

I then heard voices. At first there were just a few, but as I got closer it began to sound like there were many, maybe hundreds. Then it sounded like thousands. The stench and the air created by this tree wrought a depression that was like a choking fog. I finally had to stop because I just could not bear to go any closer. Then one of the eagles spoke up:

"This is not good!"

"Anyone can tell this is not good!" I retorted. "It would be a little more helpful to know what this is."

"This tree—it is not supposed to be like this," the young eagle said, with an obvious trembling in his voice.

"This is the result of your own impatience, ignorance, and immaturity," the old eagle interjected, who had just landed behind me.

"What happened? How is this the result of my mistake?" I demanded.

"You foolishly cut down one of the trees and did not plant the torch in its place. You know very well that every time you displace the devil or one of his strongholds, he will try to return, and if he can he will come back many times more powerful."

"I did not think about that. It is still hard to believe that one brief moment of carelessness on my part could have caused all of this!"

"The weapons we have been entrusted with are very powerful, but you must never destroy a work of the devil unless you can replace it with the works of God. If you destroy a planting of the devil you had better plant that which is of God in its place and be ready to defend it," the old eagle elaborated with obvious chastisement in his tone.

"But the eagle who was with me told me to 'go ahead' when I wanted to cut down the tree," I protested. "We both felt it was the right thing to do."

"The young eagles are here to help you and they can help you, but they are still young eagles. It does not matter who is with you or who agrees with you, you are always responsible for your own actions.

"Many who are given great knowledge do not have great wisdom. You have walked with Wisdom Himself and He abides in you. It is wisdom to inquire of the Lord before you use the authority and the weapons that He has given to you. Wisdom may still speak to you through one of us, but He will mostly speak to you through your own heart. Your obedience is to Him, not to young eagles or to old ones!"

I felt the old eagle's frustration, but I had to press him for all the understanding I could get. I was overwhelmed by the thought of having caused such a great problem.

"If I had planted the torch in its place, I would not have had it to continue touching the monuments with," I protested.

"First, you should not have cut down the tree without the command of the Lord. Then, if He commands you to do such a thing, and you have to plant the torch, you do it even if it means waiting for a time. Every time you plant this torch it will multiply. Everything planted which is the Father's will bear more fruit and multiply.

"It may seem incomprehensible to you to have to wait for that because you are so impatient, but His kingdom grows more through the patient bearing of fruit than through attacking the works of the devil. There is a time for attacking the strongholds of the devil, but that is never the main work of the kingdom.

"Remember this: You will not be judged by how many monuments you awaken, even though it is a part of your calling. Neither will you be judged by how many of these trees planted by the devil that you cut down. You will be judged on how obedient you are. Now, this lesson is over.

"We have a great battle on our hands. It is certainly wisdom that we now press on without delay. This tree is still growing and the enemy means to have this city and that cannot be allowed."

I started walking forward again. I knew that the old eagle was telling me the truth. I had foolishly used what had been entrusted to me and now I had brought on a great conflict, which had not been necessary, and one that we were not ready for.

All of the eagles were walking beside me, including the older one.

"Couldn't you be a little more helpful by flying?" I asked.

"It is hard to fly in this kind of air," one of them answered with the obvious agreement of the rest.

"Hard? Well it's hard for me to walk, but I know I must do it. Can you fight on the ground like this?"

"Not very well," the old eagle confessed. "You are right. We must fly."

With that he lifted slowly into the air and the others began to follow. They did not go far or very high and I was glad that they did not. The farther we walked, the more evil it felt. I did not want to go on. The depression grew into a gripping fear.

Soon I wanted to just abandon the whole city and start again somewhere else. If the eagles had not provided the company and covering above me, there is no way I could have continued. Even so, I was going slower and slower. Shortly I was gasping because of the great stench.

While still at a distance from the tree, I could see what was making the crashing noise. It was the fruit dropping from the tree. It was so heavy that it crashed through the roofs of buildings and houses. When it hit the street, it splattered with such force that it was like a bomb. When each one hit, a putrid fog would rise from where it fell.

Then I saw where the voices were coming from. There were great crowds of people who had come to eat the fruit. They were devouring it as if it were a delicious delicacy. It was so repulsive that I had to turn away to keep from vomiting. I felt the old eagle standing beside me.

"You had better watch this," he demanded. "You must understand what the fruit is doing to the people. Wave the sword! Hold up the torch!"

I looked down at the sword and torch I had in my hands. I had almost forgotten them and was just dragging them along. As I began to wave the sword, a gentle, refreshing breeze began to blow around us. It was like getting oxygen again.

I waved it more and more until I could see that the breeze was touching the eagles who were hovering above. With the fresh air, our vision improved quickly. Slowly confidence began to replace our fears.

I then lifted the torch as high as I could. The torch was growing brighter because of the breeze that the sword had released. Hope and resolve began to displace the depression in our group. With the sword and torch we were creating our own atmosphere.

As I looked up I could tell that the eagles all felt the thrill of flying. Great faith began rising in all of us for the coming battle. The weapons which had been given to us were greater than what we were facing. I began praying earnestly for the wisdom to use them right this time. I started to move ahead but was arrested by the old eagle who barked:

"STOP! Do not go one step further!"

I froze in my tracks. "What's the matter?" I asked, stunned a bit by the force of his command.

"You were all about to be killed. It is good to have courage, but do you not have any wisdom at all?"

"What are you talking about?" I demanded. "How were we about to be killed? What we have is obviously much more powerful than any weapon of the enemy."

"That is true, but the fruit falling from this tree could have wiped you all out at once. As I said before, we need to stand here and watch what the fruit is doing to the people. We must be sure to go only where there is no fruit about to fall."

I knew right away that the old eagle was right. I felt as foolish and immature as a child. I apologized. I could tell the young eagles all felt chastised as well.

I then began to watch the people who were the closest to us and were eating the fruit. I started waving the sword again, which I had stopped doing for just a few moments after the old eagle's rebuke. I was surprised by how foul the air had become in just those few moments.

As I raised the torch again, light came back into our eyes so that we could better see. However, it soon became obvious that the people in the fog could not see us at all. They seemed to be almost totally blind, only able to see for a few feet or so. This caused them to grope like animals for the fruit for which they seemed ravenously hungry.

As the people ate the fruit, they became pale and grew thinner. Some were gorging the fruit down as if they were starving, and the faster they ate the faster they lost weight as diarrhea was flowing from them. This was a large part of the stench, but these people did not seem to even notice it or care.

As they continued to eat, sores began to grow on them. The pain from the sores was obviously excruciating as they brushed up against one another, causing them to strike at the person they had touched. This drove the people farther and farther from each other.

We watched until those we were observing began to die. Some began to kill others who got close to them. Violence was growing and so was the paranoia and depression. I could not imagine a scene out of hell itself being any worse.

"The devil does not just like to kill, he loves to torment," the old eagle remarked. "He tries in everything he does to reduce human beings to the lowest animal state. He thinks if he can cause such humiliation to men who were made in the image of God, it is a way to mock God Himself."

It was a terrible, grotesque sight and steadily getting worse. As the depravity grew, it was soon hard to believe that these were humans.

"A pack of dogs have more dignity," I thought.

I then noticed the blood on the ground. It was being sucked into the earth as if by a slow, but powerful vacuum cleaner. As I watched, I could tell it was being drawn into the roots of the tree. The blood was its food. In the place where there was a terrible battle and much death, I looked up and could see that the branches above it were growing faster and producing more of the deadly fruit.

"We can wait no longer or the whole city will be lost," one of the eagles cried out. "We must do something."

I knew he was right, but I also knew if we had proceeded without the knowledge of what we had just observed we would not have survived our brave charge into the darkness.

I also began to feel that anyone who was working for peace on earth was doing the Lord's work. Any kind of bloodshed was feeding the root of these evil trees, which was producing this evil fruit and was increasing the evil one's grip on the earth.

"What should we do?" I asked the old eagle.

"That is why you are here," he responded. "I can give you knowledge and sometimes wisdom, but it is not my place to lead in a battle like this."

"But it was my foolishness which led to this and then I almost got us killed!" I protested. "Certainly I am not the one to lead in a fight like this!"

"Maybe you are now humble and teachable enough to do just that," the old eagle retorted, obviously resolute that he was not going to lead and I was.

I knew there was no time to argue so I just did what I felt needed to be done until an obvious leader appeared. I called all of the eagles together and organized them into two groups, appointing leaders for each one.

The first group was to fly ahead and find a path where the fruit was not about to fall. They were also to attack any fruit that they could obviously make fall prematurely. This would help clear the path more, and hopefully the premature fruit would be too unripe for the people on the ground to eat.

The second group was to go behind the first. They were to look for any fruit that had been missed or was growing so fast that it became a threat to us. I asked the old eagle to stay close to me, which he agreed to do.

As I began to walk forward, the eagles all flew ahead to do their jobs. I continued waving the sword and raising the torch. As I did this, I felt strength flowing into my arms and even my feet began to feel lighter. Soon this was purifying the air and giving light for a good distance.

This was crucial because the eagles could go no farther than the light from the torch and air from the sword, or they would choke and start getting sick.

After proceeding slowly for what seemed to be hours, we began to hear a terrible commotion in the distance. There were thousands of raging voices. A chill went through us all. I could even tell that the old eagle was growing tense. There was obviously a great battle taking place ahead.

Did we dare to continue? Who was fighting? Where was our leader? I looked back to see if anyone was coming to help us. I could not see or hear anyone, but I did notice that fruit was again falling on the path not far behind us. I just could not believe how quickly it was growing.

I also knew that we were trapped. We could not go back and we could not stay where we were. There was nowhere to go but forward, and I did not need the old eagle to tell me that.

9

THE WARRIORS

I CALLED A QUICK CONFERENCE with the leaders of both groups of eagles. They too had already seen our situation—we were now as closed in behind as we were in front, but we were also ready to keep going forward. I asked them to fly as high and as far ahead as they could and report back anything of significance that they saw just as quickly as possible.

As we moved ahead, we grew steadily closer to the clamor of a great battle. It was not long before one of the eagles came to report what they were seeing.

There was a group of about two hundred people with small swords and small lamps. Some of the swords were little more than knives, but they were brave and skilled in using them. They were fighting to hold back what appeared to be a mob, which consisted of thousands.

This little band fighting the mob had barely enough light to see, and the air they were breathing was thick with death and depression. They had built barricades and were courageously holding their ground as the mob threw the rotten, poisonous fruit at them. This fruit was so toxic that it would kill or severely wound anyone who was hit by it.

This little band was dodging it skillfully, but it was obvious that they were weary and could not hold out much longer. I was not sure what our little group could do to help against such a horde, but I knew we had to do something.

The old eagle and I approached the scene. Before they saw us, we were able to get very close to the mob because their vision was so poor. When they did see us, they began throwing the fruit at us.

They were too far away to hit us, so some of them started to run toward us. The young eagles swooped down in front of them and they stopped in their tracks, obviously terrified by the eagles.

I then took just a few steps toward them, hoping the fresh air and light from the sword and torch would awaken them from the darkness. As soon as the light and fresh air touched them, they started fleeing back into the darkness in a great panic.

One of the eagles from above dropped down to tell us the mob was just out of sight and were regrouping. For some reason they were enraged and it was obvious that they were not going to stop trying to destroy the little band.

I walked over and approached the barricade. A man and woman stepped forward who were evidently leaders. They seemed glad to see us, but wary at the same time. I told them my name and how impressed we were with their great courage.

"We know who you are," the woman replied. "Your books have helped us."

"If they have helped you, why do you feel so wary of me?" I asked.

"We are not so wary of you as much as we are of those pigeons who are with you. We're wondering why they would be with you," the man explained, obviously trying to hide his irritation, but not doing it very well.

"Those are not pigeons—they're eagles!" I shot back, trying to control my own irritation.

The man and the woman both looked at me with disbelief. I could tell they were wrestling with not wanting to insult me but wanting very much to show their scorn for the eagles. The old eagle drew me aside before I could say anything else.

"That they called us pigeons was actually a little gracious. They really wanted to call us vultures. To be honest with you, I can hardly blame them. Young eagles can make a bigger mess of things than pigeons, and even old eagles like me are very hard to be around. I think some of our younger friends here have made problems for these people before. Be patient and gentle."

"I understand," I said. "What will they think when they find out they can blame my foolishness and immaturity for this tree?"

"We have all made a bigger mess of things than most of us will ever realize in this life," the eagle responded. "Even the great saints in Scripture like Abraham, David, and even Paul the apostle, also released some great problems in the world because of their foolishness or immaturity. We are not better than they, are we?"

"No. Of course not," I responded. Realizing how true this was gave me some encouragement.

"The apostle Paul released an attitude against the church which he himself had to contend with for the rest of his life. It is by the Lord's grace that He also gives us a chance to confront and destroy the evils that we are responsible for releasing," the old eagle continued. "This is your chance with this tree. Our young eagle friends are being given another chance with these people, because like it or not, they will not survive without our help."

"This is true, but for us to get to the place where we can work together could take longer than we have, especially the way the violence is increasing out there, and how this tree is still growing," I lamented.

"They don't have to call us eagles. I don't even care if they call us pigeons, but we must find a way to work together," the old eagle replied.

As I turned back toward the couple, they seemed a little more at ease. I could tell that the waving of my sword had cleared the air some, and the torch had brightened up the whole area. As I looked over at the rest of the people, they were all looking at the eagles who were soaring nearby.

"We did not know that they were real eagles," the man and woman both stated. "I'm afraid that we did much to hurt them and drove them off because we thought they were...well...I'm very ashamed, but we actually thought that they were really vultures."

The old eagle began to speak when one of the younger ones who had landed interjected: "We are eagles, but we know what a mess we made when we were with you. We do not blame you for thinking what you did about us or for driving us away. In fact, you did the right thing. We are the ones who should be apologizing. We're all very sorry for the trouble we caused you and what we did to your congregation."

I just kept waving the sword, holding up the torch, and watching. "This is really what it means to clear the air," I thought. It was very touching but I was still surprised when I turned to the old eagle and saw tears running down his face. When he saw me he was a bit embarrassed, but apparently too happy to care very much.

"I have waited to see this for many years. There are few things more beautiful than this," he offered.

"I understand," I said, trying to make both of us feel a little more comfortable. "I suppose if I knew the whole story here I would be as moved as you are."

"If you knew the whole story you would know that we are witnessing a great miracle. In fact, it is such a miracle that it gives me confidence for this battle that we have gotten ourselves into."

"What do you mean *we*? I think I am really the one who got us into this."

"If we're going to win, we must stand together and cover each other's mistakes," the old eagle stated. "There was an eagle present with you when you did what you did, so we are all in this together. I, too, knew that it could happen, but did not go to warn you. No, we are all responsible."

The atmosphere around the little band and their barricades had obviously changed. I was surprised by how quickly the wariness I felt at first had been changed into trust with just a few apologies and a little humility.

It was obvious that we could not face what was ahead if we were fighting among ourselves. This reconciliation had to happen. I would have never dreamed it could have happened this fast. If the eagles had been offended by what they were called at first, I knew there was no way we would survive the coming battle. In fact, we could well have been fighting in two directions at once, which was sure to lead to a quick defeat.

Finally, we all turned to look toward the darkness. The falling fruit was now coming down at such a rate that it sounded like distant thunder. It seemed the darkness beyond our little area was getting darker, if that was possible. I looked at the old eagle and we both knew that we had to get going again soon.

I turned to the couple and said, "As wonderful as it has been to meet you, and for you to be reconciled with my friends here, we do not have much time. We must try to destroy the root of this tree soon or the city will be lost."

"Please, you must not leave us!" the woman cried, which was quickly followed by a chorus of many others. "You have brought us such hope and vision again. We need you and the eagles."

I looked at the old eagle and knew we were thinking the same thing. If we left these people, the hoard beyond the light would come sweeping back upon them. They were almost overwhelmed when we came to them, and they would not last long after we left.

"What can we do for them?" I asked the eagle.

"If we do not get to the root of this tree to cut it off soon, these and all of the others in this city who are fighting will be destroyed anyway. We must go on, but we can help them. Gather all of your leaders, quickly!" the eagle demanded of the couple.

While the leaders of the group were gathering, the man and woman who I had first addressed, drew me aside and began to admonish me.

"You cannot make it to the root of the tree. Just a few years ago we could walk freely anywhere in this city. Even those who hated us treated us with a little respect. But now they are all trying to either make us eat the fruit of the tree or kill us.

"There used to be many other congregations in this city like ours—some had thousands of people. There were whole movements based here with congregations all over the world. Now we are the only ones left.

"If you stay with us we can hold out. We may even take some ground back and continue to be a light to this city until the Lord returns. If you go, you will perish and so will we and there will be no witness at all in this city."

"Are you sure that you are the only congregation left in the city?" I asked.

"Quite sure. We were in fact one of the largest and strongest churches in the city. We have been reduced down to this, so I do not think that there could be any others left. If there are any others left we would have at least heard their battle. We have not heard anything in a long time, and we have not had any more join us from any of the other groups for a long time."

"We must be all who are left in this city," the woman stated. "Other churches used to be an irritation to us, but now we would give anything to know that there were others, believe me. We just don't think that there are now."

"Let's see what the old eagle has in mind," I replied. "I know eagles quite well now, and they will not do well staying in one place like this fighting behind a barricade. They would become pigeons or worse if they are made to do that kind of thing. If they are not allowed to fly, they will not be any good to you and may be just another problem, which you sure do not need right now."

"Then let them go and attack the root of the tree and you stay with us," the woman said.

I thought about this. As I looked out into the darkness, it was not very appealing to think about going out into it again. I also knew that the eagles would not be able to get far at all without the light and sword which I was carrying. There did not seem to be a solution.

"I could not let the eagles go alone," I began to explain. "They would not make it. I learned a long time ago that I could not make it far without them. In spite of the trouble they sometimes are, I no longer want to be anywhere where they are not close. I'm afraid that the eagles and I are a package deal."

"You're right," the man said. "You belong with the eagles."

"I'm sorry for even trying to separate you from them," the woman also offered, very sincerely.

I turned to the old eagle, wondering if he had any kind of solution to our dilemma. When the couple turned to him, obviously wanting to know what he thought, he began to speak.

"There is only one solution," he said. "We must all fight together until we get to the root of the tree and destroy it."

I immediately saw the wisdom in this, but I did not expect the little group to take it well. As expected, some immediately began to protest.

"We've fought for this ground for many years," one man blurted out. "You don't expect us to just leave all of this behind to follow you and the eagles, do you?"

There was silence for a few moments, as everyone seemed to consider this. Then one of the young eagles interjected.

"When we first saw the fight you were in, I had never seen such courage. I can understand how you must feel. You have fought long and hard for this ground and have obviously lost many in its defense. I certainly do not blame you for not wanting to leave.

"However, from what we can see, you would not survive another assault from the evil horde which is now surrounding you, not to mention the continued growth of this tree. There is not much left of your barricades either. I don't think any of us have a choice but to go forward. Our only hope is to put an ax to the root of that tree."

The old eagle then continued, "It is true. You could not have lasted any longer had we not come along, and we could not have gone much farther without some help. It seems that the Lord has brought us together at this time. We need each other and there seems to be only one possible choice as to what we must do."

"Of course you are right," the leader finally said. "It is going to be the hardest thing we have ever done to leave this place behind. We have paid so dearly for it, but it is obvious that we must now fight for something bigger than our little place. We must fight for the whole city and attack the root of this tree or we will have no chance to survive. We will leave our little place to follow you and the eagles."

10

THE STRATEGY

EVERYONE THEN TURNED TO LOOK AT ME. Finally the old eagle spoke up,

"What is your plan?"

"Please give me just a few minutes," withdrawing just a little to pray and seek wisdom.

I could not help but to think about the irony of this situation. I have been the major cause of this trouble, yet I am supposed to have the plan for overcoming it.

I also could not help but think of all the congregations which had been destroyed in this city and the people lost because of my immaturity and foolishness with the weapons I had been given. I grew mad at myself, but also wanted to lash out at the old eagle. I wanted to ask him why he did not come up with a plan since he was the old, wise, experienced one.

Finally a peace came over me. I knew this was not a time for bickering, and that a statement like that would only sow doubt in everyone. They did not need any more of that. I breathed a quick prayer for help and then just started talking.

"I need to know your leaders and all of the capabilities they have," I said to the man and woman leading the little band.

"I want them formed into companies according to their weapons and abilities. I will assign at least one eagle to each who will serve as their eyes. We will march and fight together, but we need to organize. Our unity and organization itself will help to push back this disorganized mob."

I then turned to the old eagle, "Get your best scouts into the air at once and have them find the weakest part of the mob where they think we can break through, and then the shortest path from that point to the root of the tree."

"Done," he replied, and immediately began sending the scouts out.

"Please report to me the information I need as soon as you get it," I said to both the old eagle and the man and woman.

"We would like to have this mature eagle come and help us determine our weapons and strengths," the woman asked, partly looking at me and partly to the old eagle.

"That is a very good idea," I responded, and the old eagle acknowledged by going with them.

I then sat down to think and pray. When I did the weight of what I had caused settled over me. I could not keep back the grief for all of the great churches which had been destroyed in this city. It had once been renowned for its culture and empire. Now I knew it was known more for the stench of this rotten tree and its fruit.

The mob had thought that the fruit was good food and they had obviously come from around the world to eat what was in fact killing them. It then occurred to me that if we succeeded in cutting it off at the root, these people would think that we had deprived them of their source of food.

"You give them something to eat," a voice behind me said. When I turned to see who it was, I was astonished.

"What are you doing here?" I said to the little girl from the valley.

"I have been fighting with these people."

"How did you get here?" I asked, still amazed to see her.

"I don't think you know me," she replied. "I understand that there are many who look like me in other places. You must be mistaking me for one of them."

"Your likeness is remarkable if you are not the same person I was thinking you were. Looking at you more closely, I can tell that there is a little difference, but you must be sisters, if not twins. And, how did you know what I was thinking?"

"Some people think louder than others. I can sometimes hear other people's thoughts. I am gifted that way so I can help people."

"I see, but you did not just hear my thoughts, you told me what to do. Where did you get that? How could I give them food to eat?"

"My gift is to know people by the Spirit, not just by appearances. This gift awakened in me when I started spending time with the eagles. That is one of the things they do best, awaken the gifts which are in others."

"How did you do that when everyone here was so offended by them?"

"I had to do it in secret, but I had to do it. Most of the younger ones here have also learned from the eagles. They taught us to hear the voice of the Lord. The Lord was the One who told me to tell you what I just did."

"You seem very sure of that for one so young," I replied. "Can you tell me more?"

"I don't really understand what I did tell you, or how you could feed those people, but I know it was the Lord who told me to tell you. One of the first things the eagles teach is that you do not need to understand to obey, but after you obey you will start to understand," the little girl replied with a disarming attitude of confidence and humility.

"As I have continued to look at you, I know that you are a teacher and a shepherd," she continued. "It is your job to give the sheep their food at the right time. The Lord must have had me tell you what I did because those people must be His sheep too. They just don't know it yet. I think it would help us to look at everyone that way. To win this fight it won't be by hurting those people, but helping them."

"You're amazing. What else can you tell me that will help me?" I asked, feeling she was certainly one who spoke for the Lord.

"I can tell you that most of the ones who are very gifted and effective in both fighting and dodging the evil are the very young ones. If our leaders would have recognized this, we would not be nearly as small as we are, but we would have many thousands."

"If the congregations that have disappeared would have understood this, they would not have died. I believe I am here to tell you that if you will choose your leaders according to their anointing and gifts, instead of by their age or appearance, you will succeed."

I knew right away that this was the word of the Lord.

"Please go, find, and bring to me the man and woman who are your leaders, as well as the old eagle," I said.

As soon as they walked up I could tell that it had not been going too well in identifying the weapons and strengths of the people who were left.

"So, you've had a hard time agreeing," I said, stating the obvious.

"Yes," the man replied. "I appreciate the wisdom and gift of such a mature eagle, but he does not know these people like I do. I have been with them for many years. Some of the things he says about them I know to be the very opposite of the way they really are. We are having a hard time agreeing on just about everyone."

"What do you say to this?" I asked the old eagle.

"It's true. I don't think we've agreed on anyone."

"Sir," I said to the man, "The main reason your congregation has become so small is not the battle that you are in, but because you have not discerned the gifts and callings of the people."

This not only stunned the man, but had obviously offended him. I waited for a minute before continuing.

"There was a time when you could gather great crowds of people. You did it in a number of ways that worked, but the times changed and you did not. You are a great leader and you have fought valiantly for the truth with remarkable endurance, but the only ones who can survive and prevail in this battle are those who spend as much time making other leaders as they do leading. This has been your weakness as well as the others—those you think of as leaders are also weak."

I could tell the man was now even more offended and wanted to argue, but restrained himself. He had been so humbled by continual defeats and was now so desperate that he was at least to a small degree open to considering that he had been wrong in some things, maybe even very wrong in his approach to both the battle and the leading of his people. As I watched him calm his own spirit down, I continued.

"Sir, please do not think I am implying that you have not done anything right. Your courage and endurance will be the foundation for which any future victory will be built upon. However, I think you must admit something very basic has not been working. Obviously, there has to be a change in the way things are done or the results will just be the same. There is a reason why you need the eagles. We must find the true leaders and raise them up quickly."

"I know you're right," the man finally offered. "I have been a failure in this and now I can see it is why we lost so many battles...and so many people. I just did not see it. I guess that is why I needed the eagles, to see what I could not see for myself. I'll do whatever you say. I know there must be a change and this is obviously it. I just hope it is not too late."

"Again, I think you are proving to be a true leader," I said. "The eagles can see, but they are not usually very good at leading. You really do need each other. For you to have the humility to acknowledge this will encourage your people, not discourage them.

"And I do not think it is too late or we would not be here. I have learned that when something seems impossible, the Lord is about to move. We have definitely provided Him with a good opportunity to move now! We need the right strategy, but more than that we need Him, His grace, and His favor. He gives grace to the humble and we need to all keep that in mind. You are probably the most genuinely humble one here. Now you must continue to lead your people, but we will help you."

"I really can see how I have missed it by not recognizing other people's gifts and letting them grow by using them," the man responded. "I also have not acknowledged the leadership that others have been given. I confess that I saw them as a threat.

"In the past, it was the gifted ones who caused the problems and the divisions. It was hard to give them more influence by letting them take some leadership. It's obvious, though, I failed even more by not letting them grow."

"Sir, if you only knew how badly I have failed and the kind of trouble my lack of wisdom and immaturity has caused, I think it would make all the trouble that either you or the young eagles have caused seem pretty mild," I replied. "Obviously we have all failed in some major ways, but I have learned that what often disqualifies us in people's eyes is the very thing which qualifies us for the grace of God.

"We're all that He seems to have here and He obviously still likes to use the foolish and weak to confound the wise and strong. Our weakness and foolishness is what I think has us here. But I also know that He does not want us to remain weak and foolish, just humble enough to seek His wisdom and His strength."

"Well said, but now we need the plan," the old eagle interjected. "Do you know how we are going to break out and attack the root of the tree? We do not have any more time to look at the past."

"I do have a plan," I responded. "First we must find the true leaders and the effective weapons which we have among us. We must then discern a point where we can break out and proceed to the root of the tree without distraction. Now go back and find the gifts and leaders who are in this group."

Looking at the man I said, "Trust this old eagle and this young girl," and I directed their attention to the girl. "She has a gift that you need."

Both the man and woman raised their eyebrows as I mentioned the gift in the little girl. They obviously started to protest and then just said, "Okay." With that they all left.

Soon thereafter, the scout eagles began to land and report. As they did, I began to think it had been a very bad idea to send them out without the old eagle. They all came back with seemingly conflicting reports. I quickly decided to just receive them one at a time, in private.

Soon it became clear that they were each seeing just a part of the whole situation, but because they were still so young they had a tendency to feel that their part was the whole picture. I felt that all of their reports were probably valuable, they just needed to be put together properly to get the whole picture.

To my dismay, after all of them had reported, I still felt I had a very incomplete picture. There had to be something that we were not seeing since I just could not believe our situation was so entirely hopeless. Not only were we completely surrounded by multitudes, with seemingly no weak points in their lines, but thousands more were joining them from every direction. They were growing in confidence and would soon come pouring in to finish off the little band, and us with them.

I then wondered about some of the conflicting reports that the scouts had brought in. One would see one part of the line as the strongest point, and another would see it as the weakest, etc. As I sat pondering this, I heard my little friend's voice behind me again.

"You don't know what to do, do you?" the little girl half asked and half stated.

"I could sure use a word from the Lord now! Do you have one for me?" I asked.

"Well, I may. I know it does not matter who is out there, but what matters is Who is in us."

"That is certainly true!" I said. "Do you have anything else?"

"I feel this means that we need to discern the gifts and callings that the Lord has given to us, and go with the strength He has given to us instead of trying to find a weakness in the enemy."

"Well! I guess that is the whole picture." I replied.

"What do you mean?" my little friend asked.

"I'll explain it to you after we are resting on a big pile of firewood from that tree," I said.

THE BATTLE

AS I HAD SUSPECTED, IT WAS DETERMINED that some of the most powerful gifts were found in the younger people, even some who were very young. Some had already learned to fight very well, using their gifts as weapons. What they lacked in training, they made up for with extraordinary faith.

The young ones did not seem to have any doubt at all about winning the battle or cutting the tree down. I knew the rest of us had very little faith that we would actually be able to do it. We were more or less going out to fight because we no longer had a choice.

I therefore decided to place some of the children and eagles with each group of adults and to fight with them side by side. I felt their main leadership at this time would be boldness and courage, which is what we really needed.

The two main words of strategy that I had been given for the battle were to make decisions based on our strengths and not the enemy's strengths. We also could not be distracted from our ultimate purpose—to cut the tree down.

Our greatest strength was the torch and the sword, which I carried, so I knew I had to go first. I did not want to hesitate, so once the people were formed into companies, we prayed, thanking the Lord for all of the great things that He had already done for us, and that He always leads us in His triumph. Then, with determination to keep thanksgiving and praise in our hearts, we started forward.

I was waving the sword like the rotor of a helicopter over my head. I was also holding the torch as high as I could. I was astounded by the wind that was being generated, knowing that my sword could not be generating all of it.

I looked back at the advancing companies and they had all drawn their swords and were doing the same thing I was. Many of the swords of the adults were chipped and gouged, and some even broken, but they had a brilliance that cast off a great light.

It was now obvious that these swords were living, seeming to come more alive from the movement. The more their holder was swinging, the more brilliant they became. The light that was coming from the entire company waving their swords was soon spectacular. As long as we did this, I was sure there was no darkness that it could not penetrate.

The wind that was being created was driving the stench of the rotten fruit away from us. The air became clear and fresh all around us. Just getting out from behind the barricades had done something to release a powerful spiritual momentum, and it was apparent that everyone was feeling it. With each step, the light and wind seemed to increase, as well as our faith. I began to think that I could not have had more confidence had I been leading an army of hundreds of thousands. I knew this little band of a couple of hundred had the power within them to do all that we needed to do.

The eagles had begun soaring above us as soon as we started. As the wind increased, they went higher and higher. After we had advanced a good distance, I was surprised we had not yet encountered the angry mob which had been surrounding the little group.

I was also surprised that none of the evil fruit had fallen on us from the branches of the tree which we were marching under. I knew this fruit was so large and toxic that it would be deadly if it hit any of us directly. However, there was no evidence that any of this fruit had recently fallen anywhere in our path. There were only some piles of what appeared to be a kind of powder lying about here and there, which the wind was blowing away. I motioned for one of the eagles to come down and report what he was seeing.

The eagle said that the evil horde had fled in terror the moment we began to march. I could understand the kind of shock it must have been for them to see this group emerge from the barricades with such light and power. Even so, I could not imagine them not regrouping and attacking us with everything they could. However, they had fled so far that the eagles could not even see them anymore.

I then asked several of them to fly as far in front of us and to the sides as possible while staying within the fresh air. When they returned, their report was even more astonishing.

The atmosphere that we were creating was killing the branches of the tree and drying up its fruit. This explained why none of it had been falling on us. What was even more amazing was how far this atmosphere we were creating had spread. We would be able to walk without danger all the way to the root of the tree.

Off to the sides, the evil horde had gathered out of reach of the fresh air, but they seemed to just be standing there dazed and milling about. They did not even seem to be eating the toxic fruit anymore, but rather seemed to have the same confused, weak, hungry look.

I gathered the leaders of the little group and explained what was happening. I knew we had to move faster to destroy the root of this tree. They agreed.

We all began to run like the wind without even getting tired. I do not know if I have ever felt such exhilaration. When we reached the root of the tree, the joy was hard to contain for everyone. Even though we had not really engaged the enemy in combat, I wondered if there had ever been a more magnificent charge or a more noble army as I looked at the faces of our little band.

The trunk of the tree was so huge that it took all of us standing at arms length from one another to surround it. As we did this, we continued to wave our swords. Then in unity we all thrust them into the trunk of the tree and it quickly died.

Its leaves began to fall like snow. The fruit that was in the branches was away from the direction that we had come and dried up quickly. The dust of this fruit created a great cloud as it was being blown away by the wind.

Then we all began to hack away at the trunk of the tree until it came crashing to the ground. Some then began to cut it up. Others went after the roots and the stump. We did not stop until there was only sawdust and firewood left. Where its huge trunk had been was a great crater, but they filled it in, and soon it looked like a freshly plowed garden.

I knew what I had to do. I planted the torch right where this great tree had stood. It took root immediately. It began to blossom right before our eyes. Then fruit appeared. I then gathered all of the people and the old eagle began to speak to us.

"This victory is worthy of a great celebration," he began. "But we do not have time for that now. Even so a story must be told so that we will fully understand what happened here. He then looked at me, and I knew what I had to do.

"This terrible thing happened because I used my sword to cut down a small tree, but failed to plant a tree of life in its place. The King has shown me mercy by letting me see my great mistake corrected. That has now been done and fruit of the Tree of Life is already growing where death so recently prevailed. By this we can remember that life is stronger than death.

"The spiritual atmosphere of a good part of this city has been changed now. On the outer edges of it are multitudes of hungry people who are now ready to eat the fruit of this tree. You must take it to them. There will be many great churches here again, all of which will be fortresses of truth and life. You must remember that you are all one."

The old eagle again interjected, "We will have eternity to celebrate our victories here. There will be a great memorial in heaven to this one. You have learned what many before you learned—that one can put a thousand to flight, and two can put ten thousand to flight (see Deuteronomy 32:30). Now you are going to learn that one can gather a thousand and two of you together can gather ten thousand.

"You are about to gather a great harvest here. Soon multitudes from all over the earth will also be coming to you. They are coming because of the light, the fresh spiritual air that is here, and the fruit of this tree. They are not coming for you or for me. We did nothing today but believe and obey. For many of us we only did this because there was no other choice. Let us not become arrogant, but humbled by what happened here.

"Even so, every one of you must now lead many. You must lead them here to eat this fruit. You must give them swords and teach them the power of the sword. You will have only led them well when they too become leaders. In this way the victory will continue to multiply. Always remember what happens when you begin to build barricades to hide behind. Now go and make disciples of the great multitudes who are now wandering around this city! They will now hear the call."

12

THE COVERING

AGAIN I AWOKE IN MY HOTEL ROOM. Even though I knew it had been a vision, it seemed very real. I wanted to write it all down quickly so that I would not forget it. It was still raining and dreary outside, but I felt energized as if I was still able to breathe some of the atmosphere of heaven.

Then suddenly I was sitting on a huge white horse. It seemed to be the one that I had found in the valley with the little girl. Even so, it seemed too big for me. I was very high off of the ground to be on a normal sized horse. Then I noticed the Lord standing next to me.

"Now you have found your seat," He remarked.

When He said this, I looked down at the saddle. It was a Western style saddle, which felt like leather with a deep purple color that was almost black. It had a golden border around its edge. It seemed to fit me perfectly and was as comfortable as an old chair.

"Lord, the saddle is perfect," I said.

I wondered how I would get on and off the horse because it was so tall. Then, as I looked at the horse's feet, I saw that they were not touching the ground, but we were hovering several feet in the air.

"This is not a normal horse," the Lord continued. "It can lift you above the earth. When you are on this horse, your journey does not have to follow the contour of the earth, but you can rise above any earthly conditions."

"Lord, is this the same horse I saw with the little girl in the valley?"

"Yes, it is the same and it is your mission. It is from the one I will ride when I return, the one that I was given by My Father. They are given to those who are preparing the way for My return.

"Many have ridden them in the past, and many must yet ride them in your time. This is the mission that has been given to you from above. When you have learned to ride this horse, you must then teach others how to ride their horses."

I thought about the little girl in the valley and the one who had just fought with us to kill the evil tree. They were already great warriors and wise far beyond their years. If there are many like them, I knew they would soon be the greatest spiritual force the world has ever known.

I also knew that this horse was capable of wonders I could not yet even imagine. I wondered what an army of children would be like if they all had horses like this.

"You live in the day of great wonders," the Lord said taking the reins of the horse in His hand and beginning to walk.

"Heaven is a place of continual marvel and awe. Those who I am about to send forth will bring many of those wonders to the earth. The children that you are about to meet are for signs and wonders and will soon go forth to My last mission on the earth before I return."

When we had gone just a few feet, we entered a great hall. There was a long line of people on either side as we passed. They were all dressed in various clothes from different eras. When we came to the center of the hall, we stopped and all of the people gathered in front of us.

"These are the ones who helped to prepare you for your purpose. You have received from their teachings or from their stories. They are your witnesses. You are representing them as you are Me, just as those you have a part in preparing will also represent you. We are all one in the great purpose of the Father— the restoration of man and the earth to their purpose."

As I sat on the horse each one of these people came up to the Lord and bowed, then looked me in the eye and gave me a word such as: "Be strong," "Be fearless," "Be gentle," "Love your neighbors," "Follow the King..."

This went on for what must have been several hours, but I would have liked for it to last longer. I felt a special bonding and impartation as I looked at them and they spoke to me. Some I was quite sure I recognized, but others I had no idea what their names were, but I still somehow knew them.

I especially watched them as they approached the Lord. It was obvious they were all His special friends and were great friends with one another. It was a glorious experience to be with them and to be spoken to by them. I had a yearning in my heart to be one of them. There was a nobility and grace upon them which was far beyond mere human elegance.

When the last one in the procession had finished, the Lord turned to me and said, "You will join them soon enough, but you have work to do first. They are not complete without you. Neither are you complete without them. This is also true of those who are to be called through you and the messengers in your time. Their words will help to keep you on the path that has been chosen for you. You can also give their words to others to keep them on their path. All of those who have life have come from Me."

Then two of them approached with a large purple cape which had the same kind of gold border as the saddle. They gave it to the Lord. He examined it and then put it on me, locking the clasp at the front. It was so large that it not only covered me but the horse's entire body.

I looked around at the crowd and then looked back at the cape. I was astonished that it was now a bright red. When I closed my eyes and opened them, it had turned into a blue more glorious than I had ever seen. I closed my eyes again and opened them and it had turned to a pure white. All of these had the same gold border.

"This is your covering," the Lord said. "It will cover you and your mission. Only here can you see it as you do now. In the realm of earth it looks very different. On earth it is very humble. This is what protects your heart, and the heart of your mission. As long as you wear this, you will walk in My grace and authority. Remember this cloak as it really is. It will protect you from the coldness of the evil times that you must walk through."

Then the Lord motioned for me to step down from the horse, which knelt low for me to do so. I knew that I should also kneel and did so. The Lord handed me the reins, as I knelt down beside the horse. Then the Lord poured oil all over my head and began to rub it into my hair like shampoo.

"This is the oil of unity," He said as He continued to rub it in.

As He did this, I felt the oil penetrate deep within my mind. Peace and clarity took the place of my usual raging thoughts, which often seemed out of my control.

Then I felt the love which I had felt just a few times before. This love caused me to love everything deeply that I looked upon. Of all of the glorious experiences I had received in the heavenly realm, this love was the most wonderful of all. I did not want the Lord to stop until this love had penetrated every cell of my being. I desperately wanted to keep this feeling. Then the Lord stopped, long before I was ready.

"This oil of unity is the anointing," the Lord started as He lifted me to my feet to look me right in the eyes.

"What I have given to you, I give to all of My people. I pour My anointing on each one to cleanse their minds. However, where you must walk on the earth there is much dust and dirt, which will be thrown at you every day. You must learn to come to Me to be cleansed again whenever your mind has been soiled.

"As you do this often, you will not be able to stand any of the filth in this world in your mind, but will love the purity and clear vision which comes only by this anointing of the Holy Spirit.

"Holiness is the nature of heaven and it must be your devotion. True holiness is true love. True love cannot come without true holiness, and true holiness always causes you to love, not condemn. You can come to Me as often as you want for this oil. As you wear it and touch others, they too will want to be clean."

13

THE COUNCIL IS CALLED

SUDDENLY I WAS STANDING IN THE VALLEY AGAIN. The beautiful little girl was still there, fighting. She was bruised, bleeding, and covered with dirt. Even so, as she looked up at me, I could see her eyes were as filled with fight and resolve just as when I had left her.

I looked down at my cloak, now a simple brown, humble fabric. Under it I saw a flash of armor. I had the sword and a flask, which contained the oil. I poured some of this on the edge of my cloak and began washing the little girl's face. She looked deeply into my eyes with a seriousness uncommon for any child.

"They are coming faster now," she started. "They are making more progress than ever before because they are not fighting as much among themselves. I do not know if we can hold this valley long without help."

"Help is coming, but I must first teach you to ride the horse," I answered.

She looked past me to the horse, which was standing just behind me. "Have you learned to ride him?" she asked.

"No, I have only sat upon him. We must learn together," I responded.

The clamor from the evil horde rose to a terrible crescendo. With that I poured the rest of my oil on her head and began to rub it in. I looked down at what should have been an empty flask but it was full again. I kept pouring it on her until she seemed to be clean. I then lifted her up on the horse and handed her the reins.

"You are going to have to learn to ride this horse in the middle of a battle," I said.

"Then I shall feel quite at home," she responded. "I don't think I have ever known a time in my life without battle."

This touched me deeply. I felt very sorry for this young girl who had already been through so much. I thought that she may truly have never known peace or rest from the struggle in her entire life. A deep desire came over me to take her away to a place where she could just be a little girl, be in a family, play little girl games...

"Don't even think about it!" A sharp, familiar, voice behind me said.

It was the old eagle. There was such a fierceness in his eyes, which seemed even greater than when he was in battle.

I also noticed the girl seemed to know him, as she did not seem at all surprised by his presence, or that he was speaking.

"There are many children who are called to a life of battle on this earth. It is their destiny, and you must not rob them of it. Those who fight here like she is doing will have a reward which they can enjoy for eternity, but here she must fight."

"Were my thoughts so far out of line?" I protested. "I was just feeling a little sorry that one so young had to go through so much. I don't think I could endure it if one of my own daughters had to go through so much. What is wrong with me feeling this way about her?"

The attention of all three of us was drawn to the clamor of the evil host which was now very near and obviously advancing. Then the old eagle looked at me with an unrelenting fierceness in his eyes which I will never forget, as he continued.

"The power that is in her is as great as the power in you. The wisdom and faith to use the power within her has in some ways been greater than yours. You will not last long in the fight without her and she also needs you.

"I warn you, do not show her pity! Self-pity is one of her greatest enemies. She cannot be defeated by the enemy if she continues to fight, but if she falls to self-pity, she will be disarmed and easily defeated."

The little girl reached out and touched my arm as she said, "He is right. Every time I start to think about myself in that way, I start to lose my faith and my courage. Please do not feel sorry for me. I know I have been given a great honor to even be able to fight in the King's battles. I gave my life to Him, and now I must live only for Him, not myself."

"I know you are both right," I conceded. "Certainly this is not the time or place for the kind of sympathy that I was feeling," I said, even though I was still a bit irritated that such a big deal was being made of my feeling a little pity for a battle-scarred little girl. The eagle did not let up.

"Self-pity is the deadly enemy of her generation. Do not open the door to that enemy by showing them pity. Give them hope! Give them courage! Teach them endurance! Give them the training, and the weapons they need, but I warn you—never, never, never give them pity! That mentality is to fear more than the evil horde out there!"

"I know an age is coming when all children will be able to play," the girl added. "I know they will be able to play with all creatures in peace and safety. Then love, joy, and peace will be the happy abode of all. I have seen this in my dreams and I have read it in the Scriptures. I am fighting so this day will come. My reward will be to see that day come. That hope is more important to me than children's games. By fighting this fight, I will live a life full of more adventure and glory than any child who dwells in a life of play and fantasy. I should be feeling sorry for them, and I do."

"Of course you are right," I confessed, now feeling very adequately chastised. "I really am going to have to become like this child to enter the kingdom," I thought to myself.

"Now we have important business," the eagle began. "The great council of apostles and elders is about to convene here. This has not happened since the first century. It will mark the beginning of the transition from this age to one which is to come. They will come together here. They are to drink from this stream for which you have been fighting."

I looked around in disbelief. It did not look very likely that anyone would be able to drink from this stream for very long, as the evil horde was already within bow shot of it and getting closer. The look on the eagle's face told me he had discerned my thoughts, but he continued as if he had not.

"When this council meets, we will not be far from the last battle in which those things that must yet be fulfilled will come to pass. Each who are coming represents streams which will water the earth. They are all seasoned warriors who have fought long and with great courage, but few of them have yet seen a victory. Many have lost their own streams and some will come here badly wounded."

"Are there no better places than this for such a council?" I asked, thinking that this was no place to bring the badly wounded or those who had never seen a victory.

The old eagle looked around carefully before answering, "No. This is the best place. I have already invited them to come and they are on their way. I expect them to start appearing very soon."

"Sir, I don't want to be talking so much when it seems that we should be fighting, but how are they going to get here? We are surrounded. And what about the badly wounded? Won't they get even more wounded here, not to mention killed?" I asked, still disbelieving that this could be the right place for such a council to be held.

"This is just as good and safe a place as where the first council met in the first century," the eagle stated. "The wounded will begin to be healed in this council. These are all great warriors. After this council they will never again retreat before the enemies of the cross. The fellowship of courage and devotion which they will find here will be their food, and the waters of life which flow through this stream will be their drink. This is the table set for them in the presence of their enemies."

Shrieks from the evil army rose to such a pitch that I could not hear the eagle anymore. A great cloud of dust rose and then descended on us so it became hard to breathe or see. I instinctively drew my sword and began to wave it. The dust retreated before it as if it were a giant fan. Soon I could see the horse, the girl, and the eagle.

We were all looking toward the continuing shrieking and clamor coming from the west. I was astonished as two, old gentlemen emerged from the cloud of dust, walking right through the evil host as if on a Sunday stroll. The horde would run at them screaming, screeching, and hurling arrows, which the old men easily deflected with their large and brilliant shields. They seemed completely unperturbed by the attacks. If they just looked in the direction of the evil ones, they retreated in a great panic. I had not seen this kind of authority in men before.

By their walk they created a large swath through the horde which did not seem to close behind them. When they came to the stream they stopped. One bowed to drink while the other stood guard. When they had both finished they continued walking up to us.

The two older men were probably in their seventies, but were extraordinarily fit. They did move a bit slowly because of their old wounds, not their age. Even so, their authority and presence was so great I felt as if an army had reinforced us.

The eagle bowed low as they stopped in front of him, and they did the same. There was an obvious mutual respect and affection between them. They then looked at the horse and girl. She dropped to the ground and also bowed. They did the same with genuine respect for her.

"We have heard much about you," one of them said to her. "No doubt you are well known not only on earth, but in both heaven and hell as well. We are very pleased to meet you."

I think it was the first time that I had seen this brilliant, little girl smile as she replied, "I never dreamed that I would actually meet you, but having you come here has made all of the battles for this place certainly worth it."

"It is mostly because of you that a great council of warriors, prophets, and wise men are about to gather here," one of the elders replied. "All who have heard of your courage and endurance have wanted to come to this place to help you. The battle will soon rage all over the earth. You have inspired those more than you will ever know to fight with courage and endurance regardless of what they face. Your friend the eagle has made you very famous. I now know just by looking at you that every word he has spoken of you is true."

As I watched the two old gentlemen, I felt almost as if I was in the presence of the King Himself. I thought if there were only a few more like them and a few more like this little girl, there would not be a battle which we could not win. Obviously hearing my thoughts the old eagle turned to look at me as he responded:

"You thought you were alone, didn't you? There are many more like these and thousands more like you. There is more evil than you are aware of too. But of this you can be sure—the King will be victorious and some of us here will still be fighting when He comes into His kingdom. The struggles we have known until now, we will soon consider skirmishes as the great battle unfolds. Blessed are those who have been chosen for the honor of fighting this great fight. Now the great wonders will begin."

"Who is this?" one of the elders said, looking toward me as he asked the eagle.

I too waited to hear his reply.

The sound of rain beating against the windows woke me up. I laid there for a few minutes listening. As I did, I could hear in the rain the sound of many feet marching. I knew the veil between the earthly and heavenly realm was getting thinner and the bridge between them was becoming stronger.

"To walk in truth, you must live in both worlds," a voice said.

I desperately wanted to return to my dream. I wanted to see the little girl again, the eagle, and the elders I had just met. Then a great sense of knowing came over me. The dream was real. I already knew or was going to meet everyone who was in my dream. I would fight in the great battle with them. All who follow the King in this time will soon know an adventure greater than any tale, greater than any dream.

14

THE BATTLE BEGINS

MONTHS LATER I SAT IN A CHAIR LISTENING to the rain beat against the windows. I could hear in it the clamor of the evil horde growing. I was again with my companions in the middle of it as the evil ones pressed in all around us. Obviously they would soon overrun the place where we stood. The two elders surveyed the scene, both continuing with a remarkable peace.

"We must make room for the others," one of the elders said as the other nodded his agreement.

"Take these vessels and fill them with water," one of them said while looking straight at the girl and I.

We did as he said. Then he told us to go and give it to those in the evil horde closest to us. The situation was so desperate that we did not have time to question his strange orders, but just obeyed, thinking that there really wasn't much to lose.

When we offered our enemies a drink it stunned them so that they stood still and a great hush came over the place. Not knowing what else to do they drank what we gave to them. They drank with such a rabid thirst that we were soon rushing back and forth for more of the water. The others around them also seemed to suddenly realize their own thirst and began begging for the water. Everyone who tasted it wanted more. Quickly we were so overwhelmed that all we could do was to direct them to the stream and invite them to drink.

Expecting them to plunge into the stream I was astonished at how they treated it with great respect, bowing down and drinking, but being careful not to even brush dirt from the banks into it.

As they drank, they changed before our eyes. The hard, tortured, demonic looks softened into human faces. They kept changing until they were like pure children again. After they were transformed they asked for vessels to take the water to the others in the evil horde. We gave them all that we had, but we only had a few. They then started fashioning containers out of their own clothes. Then some started emptying their quivers and filling them with water to take to others.

This did not entirely end the assault, as many of the divisions were not only resisting the water, but were outraged by what was happening. Even so, I knew that the valley had been saved and this would be a great victory.

I walked back to the two elders, and said, "Well it does look like this is going to be a good place to hold your council. When do you expect the others?"

"They will be here soon," the one who did most of the talking replied. "They all respond to the sound of battle and certainly they heard the clamor of this one. I'm afraid if they do not get here soon they will be sorry that they were not at least able to contribute a little to this victory."

"Who could have thought that just offering them a cup of this water would have accomplished so much?" I continued, truly amazed at what was taking place.

"The weapons of our warfare are not natural, but are divinely powerful. Their strength is in the life and nature of God. He came to give life, not take it. We overcome evil with good. We overcome by giving the life that has been given to us. Even so, this battle is far from over and the main business of this council will be how to continue until the victory is complete. We must never again stop a battle until the victory is complete. But the turning has begun. The enemy has gone as far as he can go and now we will begin to take back that which rightfully belongs to the King."

As I looked I could see individuals making their way through the evil horde that was still fighting. I knew they were the apostles, prophets, and elders who were being called to the council. They all seemed to walk in complete disregard of the threats and clamor of the evil horde surrounding them. Their walk through the midst of such evil was majestic beyond description. They stirred the horde to a frenzy, but I could tell those who had tasted of the living water marveled at this sight. The awe and respect for them was evident on the faces of the newly changed people which told me that they would be willing to follow these leaders.

"Certainly this was the beginning of a great army who would never again retreat," I thought.

"Certainly it is," a voice beside me said. "This is the beginning of what we have all been waiting for," the old eagle continued. "Just seeing this, the beginning, has made it all worthwhile."

No more words seemed possible as we all stood, knowing we were indeed on the threshold of the greatest adventure of all, but also the greatest struggle. Those who dream dreams and those who see visions would soon see their dreams and visions fulfilled.

The last battle had begun. The warriors who had been prepared for this day would all soon be mobilized. They responded to the sound of battle and the whole earth would soon hear the sound of this one.